Creative Cooking the Low Fat Way
A lifetime approach to delicious,
healthy eating.

By Yvonne Jacob

Foreword by Robert E.T. Stark, M.D.
Illustrated by Kathy Aldred
Published By
Arizona Bariatric Physicians, P.C.
444 West Osborn Road, Phoenix, Arizona 85013
602/ 248-7852

First edition — 1989

ISBN: 09618415 - 3 - 2

Library of Congress Catalogue Number: 89-091303

This book is for David, with all my love.

Special thanks to Dr. Stark, Kalindi, Mimi, Keith, Tobias, and Martha for all of the love and support you have given to me while I have been writing this book. Special thanks also go to my editor Jo Girard for her many helpful suggestions and comments, and to Rose Arnold, who helped me so much with the overall design of the book. I would also like to thank my illustrator, Kathy Aldred for her great illustrations, and valuable input into the project.

Table of Contents

Your Notes:

Foreword

There is at present a general consensus among health authorities in the United States as well as the American Heart Association and the American Cancer Society that the average American food intake is too high in fat content. This high intake of dietary fat is associated with increased risks for obesity, some types of cancer, especially breast and colon cancer, and possibly gallbladder disease. Obesity increases the risk for high blood pressure and stroke, adult onset or Type II (non-insulin dependent) diabetes mellitus, coronary artery disease, gall bladder disease, cancers of the uterus and breast in women and cancers of the colon and pancreas in men. Epidemiologic studies have consistently demonstrated that excess weight is also associated with an overall risk for death and this risk increases as the severity of obesity increases.

The association between high fat intake and medical problems which represent the leading health threats for Americans is comprehensively discussed in the 1988 Surgeon General's Report on Nutrition and Health. This Report states that "the primary priority for dietary change is the recommendation to reduce intake of total fats, especially saturated fat, because of their relationship to the development of several important chronic disease conditions. Because excess body weight is a risk factor for several chronic diseases, maintenance of desirable weight is also an important public health priority."

The Surgeon General's Report states that dietary fat in the United States accounts for about 37% of total caloric intake. Other recent studies state that the percentage of fat calories to total calories in the American diet is over 40. It is quite easy to exceed this figure. For example a "Big Breakfast", a standard salad lunch and a "Double Cheeseburger" dinner will total around 2800 calories of which 59% are fat calories. The standard for maximum fat intake which has been adopted by the American Cancer Society, the American Heart Association and by just about every authority in human nutrition in the United States is 30% Fat Calories, i.e., not more than 30% of our daily calorie intake from foods and beverage should come from fat.

Keep in mind that the standard for maximum fat intake is expressed in terms of Percent Fat Calories rather than in terms of total fat calories, total fat grams or percent fat grams. Unfortunately, there is a serious problem with the 30% Fat Calorie standard; it is quite difficult to comply with it. One way would be to add up the day's fat calories in meals and snacks and divide by total calories (Fat Calories divided by Total Calories equals % Fat Calories). There are some formidable obstacles to this method of computing % Fat Calories including the lack of readily available information about the fat calorie content of foods and the time consuming effort to keep track of both fat and calories.

One of the virtues of Yvonne Jacob's new book "Creative Cooking the Low Fat Way", is that all of the recipes are truly low fat in that the fat content is below the 30% Fat Calorie Standard for maximum fat intake. The 30% standard is a dividing line which separates lean foods from fatty foods, lean meals from fatty meals, and lean recipes from fatty recipes. Each of Yvonne's recipes provides information which is rarely if ever provided in conventional recipe books, namely, how each recipe measures up to the 30% Fat Calorie Standard.

A second virtue of "Creative Cooking the Low Fat Way" is that all of the recipes have been tested for taste. Yvonne has demonstrated that low fat content recipes can result in delicious as well as healthy meals and snacks. Her book is an important contribution to the literature on food preparation for health.I know that you will enjoy having Yvonne with you as you utilize her unique recipes with the confidence that they will assist you in your goal of controlling fat for health.

Robert E.T. Stark, M.D.

Dr. Stark is past president of The American Society of Bariatric Physicians (doctors who treat obese patients and their associated medical problems). He is the author of "Controlling Fat For Life" and "The Percent Fat Calorie Tables". His publications have been featured in Reader's Digest, Prevention, Shape, Esquire and Redbook magazines, medical journals and national television programs.

Introduction

In July 1988, surgeon general Dr. C. Everett Koop, threw his weight behind a new report on nutrition and health, and urged Americans to cut down on fat intake, especially saturated fat and cholesterol. Koop claimed overconsumption of fat to be "the greatest concern", because high fat diets have been linked with diseases such as cancer of the breast, colon, rectum, and prostate. A high fat diet also contributes greatly toward obesity, which in turn contributes to many diseases, such as heart attacks, strokes, and hypertension.

Both the American Heart Association, and the American Cancer Society recommend that we keep our fat intake down to 30% or less. At present Americans eat about 37% of their daily calories in the form of fat, and in many cases this figure is much higher.

All of the recipes in this book are 30 percent fat or less, and have been tested for taste, and ease of preparation. Since the majority of people who will use this book are out working all day, I felt it was important that the recipes be as simple as possible to prepare. Most of us do not have the time or desire to spend long hours in the kitchen, and yet wish to come up with a good tasting, nutritious meal as quickly as possible. Advice is given on how to cut down fat. Information on choosing meats, and selecting vegetables are also included in the book. There is a section on reading labels, and also a section on commonly used herbs. Nutritional information has been calculated using a computer program, and nutrient values are given for every recipe, including calories, protein, carbohydrates, total fat, cholesterol, fiber, and percent fat calories.

Fat does leave a satisfying taste on the tongue, and it is necessary to replace this taste by using items such as fresh herbs, spices, and high quality, low fat ingredients. The end result of using ingredients such as these, is a satisfying, lighter tasting meal. Merely removing the good taste we experience from fat, and not replacing this taste with another flavor, makes it very difficult for people to enjoy low fat food for any great length of time.

The purpose of this book then, is to give people a head start on the road toward a good tasting, low fat, lifetime eating program. This book is not a "quick weight loss diet", but by following the recipes in this book, you will lose weight the way that is recommended by most medical authorities — slowly and steadily. You will not feel that you are being deprived, (there is even a chocolate pound cake recipe), and you will not find that it is necessary to cheat if you have to cook for a special occasion, since there are many recipes included that are suitable for entertaining.

I have taught cooking for many years and am a member of the International Association of Cooking Professionals, and I was quite resistant to change my cooking style to one that is low fat. Frankly it is a lot easier to make a dish taste good, using liberal amounts of oil and butter.

The evidence is overwhelming, however, that a high fat diet can actually shorten our lives. Why continue to ignore the evidence? We are the greatest nation in the world, but unfortunately not the healthiest. A tremendous amount of money is spent on health care, and the loss to industry through health related problems is now significant. It is every individual's responsibility to take charge of his or her own nutrition, and in most cases people experience much better health if a well balanced, low fat diet is followed.

This book then is a contribution toward helping Americans become healthier. It is meant to be used, not stuck on a book shelf. There is space in the margins for making notations of any changes that you wish to make. Write in it, use it as a guideline for creating your own recipes, have fun cooking from it, and above all else enjoy eating the recipes you prepare from it!

Here's to your health!

Yvonne Jacob

Yvonne Jacob

Easy Ways To Reduce The Use Of Fat

Every time you reduce the fat in your diet it is comparable to trimming the fat right off your hips or waistline! As you reduce the fat in daily eating, the pounds will begin to fall away. Many times the fat can be reduced without any noticeable difference in taste, and it all adds up. By reducing your use of butter or margarine only 1 tablespoon a day, for example, could help you lose 10 pounds in 1 year!

Shopping

SHOP WISELY AND NEVER GO GROCERY SHOPPING WHEN YOU ARE HUNGRY! By shopping wisely you can leave a lot of fattening items behind in the store. The calories that don't go into your shopping cart won't end up being eaten at home.

❖ Choose lean cuts of meats, and try to buy more chicken and fish. If you buy a whole chicken or turkey, make sure it is not the self-basting kind which has been injected with fat, often the saturated kind.

❖ Buy nonfat yogurt and milk.

❖ Use reduced-calorie or low fat salad dressings and soups.

❖ If you do not already whip your own butter or margarine, buy the whipped kind or low fat.

❖ Eliminate white breads and cereals, and replace them with whole wheat or stone-ground breads, muffins and rolls. Whole-grain cereals, and cereals with bran or high fiber are a wiser choice.

❖ Bring home plenty of fresh fruit and green leafy vegetables. Besides being loaded with fiber and important vitamins and minerals, these items will take the place of many high fat foods.

Cooking

REDUCE THE FAT in cooking whenever possible as follows:

❖ Avoid frying food. Not only is fried food very fattening, but it has been suggested that chemicals which are possible cancer-causing may form when food is charred or fried in hot oil.

7

❖ Boiling, steaming, sautéing in a little oil or butter, baking, roasting (using a rack), poaching, broiling and stir-frying are all good cooking methods that require little or no fat.

❖ Use non-stick spray when recipe calls for a dish to be buttered, and also spray your stick-resistant or non-stick cookware.

❖ Good quality, heavy pans are one of the best ways to cut down on fat without burning the food, and also the food cooks evenly.

❖ Reduce the amount of butter, margarine, or oil in a conventional recipe by half. Add stock or wine if extra moisture is needed instead of more fat.

❖ Make stocks and soups in advance and allow them to chill well in the refrigerator. The fat will solidify on the top and will be easy to remove. If you are making stocks, soups, stews, or gravies that will be eaten the same day, be sure to remove the excess fat.

❖ Choose only the leanest of meats, and trim off all visible fat. Remove skin from poultry. There is a 20% transference of fat from chicken skin to the meat during cooking!

❖ Cut down your intake of salt by using herbs (fresh whenever possible) and spices, lemon juice, garlic, ginger, spicy sauces and seasonings.

❖ Puree fresh vegetables and use as a light refreshing sauce instead of the traditional butter-based sauces.

Baking

❖ Be aware of the fat or oil content in desserts, and choose recipes with the lowest amount.

❖ You can replace half of the egg yolks called for in a recipe by using 2 egg whites. For example, if the recipe calls for 2 eggs, use 1 whole egg plus 2 egg whites. This works well with most recipes.

❖ One mashed banana can be substituted for 1 whole egg.

❖ Replace sour cream with non-fat yogurt or lite sour cream.

❖ Use low fat milk instead of whole milk.

❖ Instead of double crusted pies, make fruit crisps or crumbles.

Serving

❖ You can eat fewer calories without eating less food! One pint of strawberries, for example contains only 97 calories and 11% fat. On the other hand, high-calorie high fat foods are easily and quickly eaten. One tablespoon of butter is 100 calories and 100% fat. Now which item would you choose?

❖ Use smaller plates that are subdued in color. Large plates need large servings, and bright colors tend to make us feel more hungry.

❖ Reduce the size of meat portions. Serve more fish, poultry, and dried bean dishes.

❖ Serve more whole grains, and fresh fruits and vegetables. High fiber foods satisfy the appetite for a much longer period of time than sweet sugary foods.

Many high fat foods are also high in sodium. By reducing your dietary fat you will also be reducing your sodium intake as well.

Time Saving Hints For Healthy Cooking

Food Processors

One of the best investments you can make toward easier cooking is the purchase of a food processor; you can save lots of time in preparation. Food looks better, when all of the slices are uniform in size, and also the food cooks more evenly, because the slices are all the same thickness.

Keep your food processor on a kitchen counter, or you will find that you will not use it!

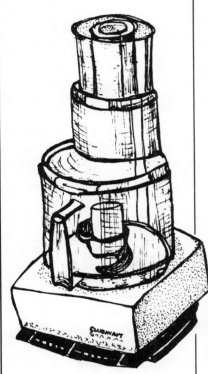

1. When slicing onions, slice extra and freeze in a plastic freezer bag for use as needed, this can also be done with green and red peppers.

2. Make up large quantities of stocks and freeze in plastic containers. Freeze some in ice-cube trays, and then bag these stock-cubes for use in sauces or when only small amounts are needed.

3. Chop up some fresh herbs that you frequently use, such as parsley or chives, and freeze in tiny well sealed containers.

Preparing Foods Ahead

1. When preparing sauted vegetables that you use frequently (such as onions or mushrooms), consider sauteeing extra for freezing. Freeze in freezer bags.

2. Next time you make muffins or pancakes, mix up one or two extra batches of the dry ingredients and store in a plastic bag in the refrigerator for a super fast fresh breakfast later in the week.

3. When you find that you have accumulated onions, carrots, or even other mild flavored vegetables, consider making a large batch of vegetable stock. Vegetable soups also freeze well, and make a quick lunch or light dinner.

Knives:
Good knives should be stored in a knife block. Never throw them in a drawer in a jumble with other utensils. Do not put them in a dishwasher either, as this will dull the blade.

Cooking Utensils

Good quality cookware is a worthwhile investment, and results in better tasting, more evenly cooked food.

Use heavy quality non-stick or stick resistant pans. This really will help you use a lot less fat. Spray the pan very lightly with a cookware spray also.

Good quality knives will make any chopping or dicing that you do, much easier and faster.

12

The Healthy Cook's Kitchen

Is your kitchen armed to fight fat? Having the right cooking equipment can go a long way toward helping. Following is a list of kitchenware that can be a real boon to you:

Refrigerator and Freezer space. Adequate refrigerator space is a real work saver, especially if you don't have the time for frequent shopping trips. You will be using more fresh fruits and vegetables, and will be discovering more creative ways to use leftovers as you learn to cook the spa cuisine way.

Food Processor. This is a really fabulous tool! It not only saves time in the preparation of foods, performing chores such as chopping, dicing, slicing, and pureeing with remarkable speed, but it can also be used for making items such as breads, cookies, cakes and muffins. If you have to choose between a food processor or a mixer, choose the food processor.

Blender. If you have a food processor you don't really need a blender, unless you make a lot of fruit puree type drinks. These whip up better in a blender and are also easier to pour and serve.

Fat Mop. This handy gadget has a head that is made of absorbent plastic fibers. The grease adheres to the mop as you swish it through the stock or stew. The mop is washable.

Egg Separator. If you are uncomfortable separating yolks from whites, this inexpensive gadget will save you many mishaps.

Grater. Even if you have a food processor you will find that you will need one of these. Small quantities of shredded vegetables and/or cheese are used often in this type of cooking.

Miscellaneous Gadgets. Any gadget that will make your cooking easier or more fun is a good investment. An ice-cream machine, which can be used for making low fat frozen yogurts, or sorbets would be a wise buy for someone giving up an ice-cream habit .

Knives. Good, sharp knives are essential for trimming the fat from meat, slicing meats very thin, and for preparing fresh fruits and vegetables easily and quickly. Never buy a knife without first handling it yourself. Knives should feel well balanced in your hand, and should be stored in a knife block. Good quality knives should never be put in the dishwasher. The heat of the dishwasher does strange things to the blade: it makes the steel molecules go crazy, thus dulling and weakening the knife.

Measuring cups and spoons. All measurements given in this book are level. Liquid measurements should be measured in a liquid measuring cup. Do not measure dry ingredients, such as flour, in

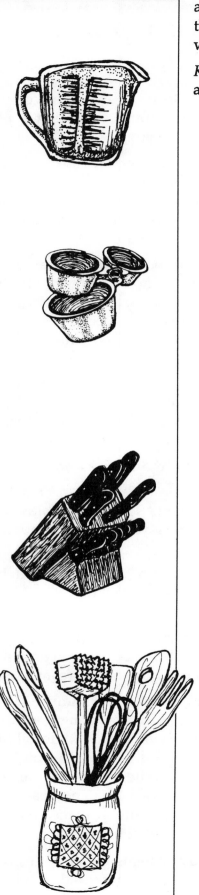

a liquid measuring cup. Dry ingredients should be measured in the cup size indicated in the recipe and then leveled off smooth with the flat side of a knife.

Kitchen Scale. This is really handy for weighing serving portions and many other basic ingredients as well.

Wrapping It Up With Labels

Being knowledgeable about the information printed on food labels, is a very important factor regarding your health.

Who approves the label?

The U.S. Department of Agriculture's (USDA) Food Safety and Inspection Service (FSIS) approves labels for all products that contain at least 2% poultry or 3% meat. This is part of the Federal meat and poultry inspection program. Labels for other products are approved by the U.S. Food and Drug Administration.

Seven things must be on the label before a product is approved.

1. The product name

2. A list of its ingredients

3. Its weight

4. The official USDA inspection stamp

5. The number of the plant where it was produced

6. The producer's or distributor's name and address

7. Handling instructions if the product is perishable.

Many manufacturers include more information on the label. You may see handling, storing, and cooking directions, for instance. Some even have cooking tips, suggested menus, and nutrition information.

Giving the product a name

USDA sets standards for how much meat and poultry must be used in items using certain names. For example, "Beef with Gravy" must contain at least 50% cooked beef, while "Gravy with Beef" contains only 35% cooked beef. Meat and poultry processors may add more meat than the required amount, but if less is added then the product must be given a different name.

The picture on the label strongly influences the buyer, so it must be honest. If the label shows five slices of beef, at least five slices must be inside. And when a picture shows fancy extras that are not part of the product, such as cranberry sauce or lemon slices, they must be identified as "suggested servings."

USDA standards also limit the amount of fat, moisture, and other ingredients that can be added to meat and poultry products.

What's in the product?

All ingredients in the product recipe must be listed in the ingredients statement on the label. The main ingredient comes first. Others, including additives, follow in order of weight.

Additives such as natural spices and flavorings can be listed as a group, i.e., spices or flavorings. However preservatives, artificial flavorings or colors, and other additives must each be named.

Why additives are used in meat and poultry products.

Additives have been used in food throughout history. Salt has long been used to preserve meat. Sugar and corn syrup are also widely used. Additives serve many purposes in food. They prevent salad dressing from separating, salt from becoming lumpy, and packaged goods from spoiling on the grocery shelf. They also give margarine its yellow color and keep cured meat safe to eat. But before an additive can be used in a meat or poultry product, it must be approved by the USDA.

Consumers who must avoid certain substances in their diets can read product labels and learn the names of additives. On some labels, the purpose for these ingredients may also be listed. The chart on the following pages lists some of the approved additives that can be found in meat and poultry and the purpose for their use in these products:

Commonly Used Additives

Functions in Foods	Some Commonly Used Additives	Foods in Which Additives are Used
Acidifiers increase acid levels in products to improve flavor and texture	Acetic acid (vinegar) Citric acid Lactic acid Phosphoric acid	Fresh and cooked sausage
Antioxidants prevent rancidity	BHA/BHT Butylated hydroxyanisole TBHQ (Tertiary butylhydroquinone) Propyl gallate	Fresh pork, beef, and Italian sausages; some beef patties; margarine and oleomargarine.
Binders thicken ingredients and extend product	Isolated soy protein Dry whey Sodium caseinate Algin	Sausage, imitation sausage, some meat loaves, soups and stews Breading mixes and sauces
Curing Agents improve color and taste	Sodium nitrite Sodium ascorbate	Frankfurters, salami, bacon, bologna, ham, and other cured meat and poultry products.
Flavoring Agents impart desired flavor	Corn syrup Dextrose	Sausage, frankfurters, meat loaf, luncheon meat, and chopped and pressed ham.

Dates and Handling Instructions

Many products have dates on them, even though dating is optional. The date stamped on product packages can indicate product freshness and can serve as a guide to safe storage time, provided consumers know how to use it.

What do they mean?
The *"Sell-by"* date is the last day the product should be sold.

The *"Use-by"* date tells you how long the product will retain top eating quality after you buy it.

Some products have an *"Expiration Date"*. which tells you the last day the food should be eaten or used.

Canned and packaged foods have *"Pack"* dates which tell you when the product was processed.

Following handling instructions is the best way to ensure that products remain safe to eat. Today the packaging of products that need to be refrigerated is similar to packaging for products that need to be stored on the shelf. Therefore, it is necessary to follow the directions on the label to make sure you handle the product properly.

All perishable products must give handling instructions, such as *"Keep Frozen"* or *"Keep Refrigerated."* Some meat and poultry products may be labeled *"Ready to Eat"* or *"Fully Cooked,"* which means no further cooking is necessary. Other product labels may have directions on how long and at what temperature to cook a product. These directions are not required or verified by the USDA. When cooking instruction are not included on the label, your best bet is to cook the product thoroughly.

Labeling Dictionary

Binders and extenders - help to hold a meat or poultry product together and also aid in retaining product moisture.

Curing - is often done by adding a limited amount of nitrite in combination with salt during processing. These curing ingredients give products such as bacon and turkey ham, their characteristic taste and color.

Skeletal Meat - refers to muscular tissues that remain attached to the animal's bone structure when muscles used for major meat cuts are removed.

Meat Byproducts (also called "Variety Meats" - are edible animal parts other than the muscle and skeletal meat. When variety meats, such as organ meat, are used in products, the term "Meat Byproducts" or "Variety Meats." are included in the product name.

Rancidity - occurs when fat is exposed to oxygen. Exposure to oxygen causes fat molecules to break down quickly resulting in a stale, rancid odor in the product. Antioxidants, such as BHA and BHT are used to slow this process and extend the shelf-life of meat and poultry products.

How Nutritious Is It?

While more and more labels are providing nutrition information for consumers, this is not usually required for meat and poultry products. Products bearing special claims however, are an exception.

Here are some popular claims that might be seen on meat and poultry products.

❖ *Natural* - means that the meat or poultry product is minimally processed and that it contains no artificial flavors, colors, or preservatives.

❖ *Imitation* - is used on products made to resemble or substitute for other products. Imitation sausage for instance must appear on products that look like sausage, but do not contain the specific ingredients required by USDA product standards.

❖ *Irradiation* - is a newly approved process for controlling certain microorganisms in some meat products. Irradiated foods must be labeled "treated with radiation," and the irradiation logo must show on the label.

❖ *Low-Calorie* - must prove its value to dieters. To do this, some manufacturers list the calories, protein, carbohydrates and fat in a single product serving. This is called the short nutrition list.

❖ *Sodium Free - or* "Salt Free" products must contain 5 milligrams (mg.) or less sodium per serving.

❖ *Very Low Sodium* - products must contain 35 mg. or less sodium per serving.

❖ *Low Sodium* - Low sodium products must contain 140 mg. or less sodium per serving.

19

❖ *Unsalted or No Salt Added* - products processed without salt. CAUTION: These products may contain other sources of sodium such as monosodium glutamate. Check the ingredient statement.

❖ *Reduced Sodium* - products must contain 75% less sodium

❖ *Lower or Less Salt or Sodium* - products contain at least 25% less sodium than the traditional product.

❖ *Extra Lean* - products must contain 5% or less fat. The actual amount must be indicated on the label.

❖ *Lean and Low Fat* - products must contain 10% or less fat. The amount of fat must be indicated on the label.

❖ *Lite, Lighter, Leaner, and Lower Fat-* products must contain 25% less fat than similar products on the market.

❖ *Sugar Free* - may mean that the product contains honey or artificial sweeteners. Sugar may also be listed as sucrose, glucose, fructose, corn syrups, corn sweeteners, maltose, or dextrose.

How To Figure Percent Fat Calories

To figure percentage of calories from fat: Multiply grams of fat per serving by 9 calories (there are 9 calories in 1 gram of fat). Divide the fat calories by calories per serving, then multiply by 100. This gives the percent of fat or percent fat calories. The goal is to reduce percentage of calories from fat to 30.

Many items in the grocery store appear to be low in fat but in reality are not. A good example is 2% low fat milk. The 2% refers to the fat content by weight. NOT the percentage of calories from fat. To figure out the percent fat calories of 2% milk, we take the grams of fat in a serving which are 5, multiply by 9, which gives us 45. Divide by the number of calories which is 120. This gives us .375 which we now multiply by 100 which is 37.5%. So now we discover that the milk we thought was 2% fat is in reality over 37%; much too high!

Turkey products are not always low fat either. Again their manufacturers tout their fat-free content, but that's by weight, not the percent of calories from fat. One example of a turkey pastrami says "95 percent fat free." In reality it takes 36 percent of its calories from fat. When calculations are done on some other packages, turkey ham is shown to be 51 percent fat calories, while a brand of regular ham is 36 percent.

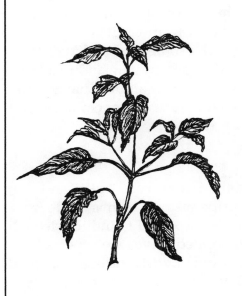

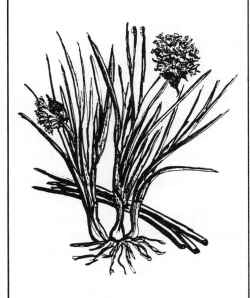

Cooking With Herbs

From ancient times herbs have been cultivated for culinary purposes, and throughout the centuries cooks have developed the art of combining and contrasting the different flavors to bring out the best in a favorite dish. For many years the use of herbs was sadly neglected, but now they are finally making a comeback, and are extremely valuable in low fat cooking. Herbs are at their best in light wholesome dishes of this sort, and their addition to our diet adds only flavor, vitamins, and minerals — without calories or fat.

Some of the most popular herbs, folklore, and suggestions for their use are given here.

Basil

Basil is one of the most relished herbs, and has been popular in cooking and perfumes for over two thousand years. Some authorities say that the name basil comes from the Greek word for king; others say that it is linked with the fabled reptillian creature Basilisk. In medieval Europe, a basil leaf was thought to be a passport to heaven. Basil does make an excellent dried herb, and its sweet-and-spicy flavor is good in soups, marinades, vinaigrettes, grain dishes, omelets, and tomato sauces. Fresh basil, however, is far superior, and the results are very different when using it fresh. Fresh basil is the main component of pesto sauces, and has a special affinity with fresh tomato salads, seafood salads, and chicken and fish dishes. Both fresh and dried basil are good in vegetable dishes such as eggplant, onions, peas, squash, spinach, and tomatoes. Always use fresh basil whenever you can, and handle the leaves with care, even the slightest bruise will blacken them. Basil grows well in a window box, and is supposed to repel flies. The leaves can be frozen in polythene bags.

Chives

Chives are a member of the lily family, whose relatives include garlic, scallions and onions. One form of chives was cultivated in ancient China and was used throughout Asia. The plants are easy to grow in a pot by a sunny window, year round, and their pretty lavender blossoms which can be used as a garnish for salads and soups, should be cut off to keep the flavor in the leaves. The flavor of chives is similar to scallions, yet more delicate. Fresh chives add flavor to baked potato along with nonfat

yogurt, and almost any fresh vegetable salad. Fresh and dried chives can be used in dips, dressings, soups, and sauces. When cooking with them, use the dried form at the beginning of the cooking time, and the fresh at the last moment.

Cilantro:

Cilantro is not available in dried form, since its aroma, and pungent flavor seem to dissipate when dried. Sometimes referred to as Spanish or Chinese parsley, this is the same herb whose seeds are the spice corriander. Its unique flavor and aroma are enjoyed by some, and disliked by others. It is widely used in Mexican, Indian, and to a lesser extent Oriental cookery. Cilantro adds an unusual zest to pinto bean stews, tacos, tomato sauces for enchiladas, and curried vegetables.

Dill Weed:

The name dill comes from the Saxon word "dilla" and means to lull. In England gripe water which is made from seeds, is given to babies for hiccups and to induce sleep. It is so mild it is quite safe. Chopped leaves are especially good with cucumber salads and yogurt, and are also good in hot or cold soups, omelets, and with yogurt cheese or cottage cheese.

Marjoram and Oregano:

The Greeks and Romans thought that marjoram presaged happiness, and its Latin name origanum means joy of the mountains. Wild marjoram is sometimes called oregano, and the two can be used interchangeably. Marjoram is slightly sweeter, and stronger, and should be used more sparingly. Marjoram is an important ingredient in the seasoning of meat, poultry, fish, soups, stews, and stuffings. It is also used in conjunction with other dried herbs to flavor vegetable dishes, Italian-style tomato sauces, pizza sauces, bean stews, grain dishes, and salad dressings.

Mint:

The Romans grew mint as an aid to digestion, and the Pilgrim Fathers brought mint with them to America. According to Greek legend Menthe was a nymph loved by Pluto, and Proserpine in a jealous rage changed her into mint. Mint blends well with crushed garlic and cucumber when added to yogurt cheese or cottage cheese mixtures. The chopped leaves are wonderful over steamed carrots or

24

peas, and there is no substitute for fresh mint in summer beverages, or as a garnish for fresh strawberries, melons and fruit salads.

Parsley:

Parsley has one of the longest recorded herbal histories. The Greeks and Romans wove it into the crowning garlands for their heroes and the Romans thought so highly of its strengthening abilities, that their horses and soldiers ate it daily.

Parsley is rich in vitamin C and A, with good amounts of B,D, and E. It has as much vitamin A as cod liver oil, and more vitamin C than oranges. It also contains phosphorus, sulphur, and potassium, and is rich in iron and calcium. Too often parsley is used as a garnish and set aside, instead of being eaten for its health giving properties.

Parsley just doesn't translate well into dried form, and it is best to only use fresh, since it is readily available year-round. Use this fresh, mild herb in salads, salad dressings, soups, bean dishes, casseroles, vegetable dishes, chicken and fish dishes, omelets, and herb breads. Italian parsley has a stronger flavor, and is preferred by many for cooking.

Rosemary:

Rosemary has a well-known legacy as the emblem of everlasting love, friendship, and remembrance. It is traditionally woven into bridal garlands, and also used to be burnt in sickrooms to purify the air. Rosemary needs to be used sparingly, since it has a strong flavor that can be overwhelming. It is an excellent herb with chicken, grilled fish, vegetable stews, and tomato soups and sauces.

Sage:

Sage symbolizes wisdom and immortality, and has been used since the time of the Romans. Its name has been translated as "to save", "to heal", or "I am well". Sage can be used sparingly in salad dressings, rice pilafs, pumpkin or squash soups, baked fish, turkey, and stuffings.

Savory:

Savory comes in summer and winter varieties that can be used interchangeably. Summer savory is more widely available, since it is an annual plant, and has a milder sweeter flavor. Summer savory was popular with the

25

Greeks and Romans who used it in highly spiced sauces. The early American settlers brought both varieties with them to the New World. Savory is a useful seasoning that tastes like a cross between parsley and thyme. It is known as the bean herb, since it has an affinity with beans. Try it in bean soups and stews, soups, salad dressings, baked or with broiled fish, turkey dishes, and chicken.

Tarragon:

The French call tarragon the king of herbs, and it has a sharp-sweet, aniselike flavor and scent. Tarragon adds a distinctive touch to salads and fresh green vegetables, such as peas, asparagus, and green beans. Tarragon is excellent in fish and chicken dishes, makes ordinary mayonnaise special, and adds an exceptional touch to tomato, and egg dishes. Tarragon is probably best known for its role in making an elegant vinegar.

You can make your own tarragon vinegar by putting 2 ounces of tarragon leaves in a bottle, and adding 2 1/2 cups of wine vinegar. Cap the bottle and strain after it has set for 4 weeks.

Thyme:

The herb thyme took its name from the Greek for fumigate, and the ancient world used it as an antiseptic. In days of old, ladies embroidered a symbolic sprig of thyme and a honey-bee on their scarves, which they gave as "favors" to the bravest knights. Thyme can be added to soups, stuffings, vegetarian dishes, fish dishes, stews, salads, and eggs. Bees love thyme, and thyme honey is very good.

Safeguard Nutrients in Foods

It is important to store and cook food correctly to prevent the nutrients from being destroyed.

❖ Frozen foods should be stored at 0 degrees or below. At 15 degrees F frozen vegetables stored for 6 months loose half their vitamin C.

❖ Vegetables should be cooked in a small amount of water. Boiling vegetables in large amounts of water leaches vitamins and minerals into the cooking water. Vegetables can also be stir-fried or steamed. Try to use the remaining water in a recipe or else drink it.

❖ Vegetables should be cooked just until crisp-tender.

❖ Leftovers should be refrigerated, covered. They should be used within a few days otherwise half of their vitamins can be lost.

Salad Dressings, Sauces and Toppings

Salad dressings, sauces, and toppings, can add a huge amount of fat to your diet. To reduce the amount of fat in the dressings that you usually make, try substituting nonfat yogurt or buttermilk for the mayonnaise you would usually use, and experiment with different fresh herbs, or herb mustards, for added flavor. Herb vinegars are an excellent choice for oil and vinegar dressings, and substituting half of the oil with water or juice will dramatically lower the fat in these types of dressings.

Salad Dressings, Sauces and Toppings

Spicy Italian Dressing

This low fat recipe is a good substitute for the traditional oil-based Italian dressing.

Serves 8

2 cloves garlic
1 tablespoon fresh basil or 1 teaspoon dried
1 tablespoon fresh oregano or 1 teaspoon dried
2 cups tomato juice
1 tablespoon chopped scallions
2 teaspoons horseradish
2 teaspoons Worcestershire sauce
2 tablespoons red wine vinegar
salt and pepper to taste

Method

Blend all ingredients until smooth.

Nutrient Values:

Calories:	13.9	Cholesterol:	0 mg
Protein:	0.590 g	Fiber:	0.580 g
Carbohydrates:	3.49 g	% Fat Calories:	4
Total Fat:	0.073 g		

Sesame Oriental Dressing

Try this salad dressing sometime when you are planning an Oriental dinner. It can also be used for leftover chicken as a dressing to make an Oriental chicken salad.

Serves 6

1 1/2 cups plain nonfat yogurt
2 tablespoons chopped fresh parsley
2 tablespoons chopped fresh chives
2 tablespoons lowfat mayonnaise
2 tablespoons Dijon mustard
2 tablespoons low sodium soy sauce
1 tablespoon fresh ginger

Method

Combine all ingredients in a bowl, and mix well. Chill at least 1 hour before serving.

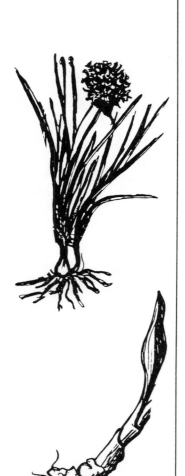

Nutrient Values:

Calories:	52.1	Cholesterol:	2.21 mg
Protein:	3.88 g	Fiber:	0.139 g
Carbohydrates:	6.34 g	% Fat Calories:	23
Total Fat:	1.32 g		

Buttermilk Herb Dressing

Much lower in fat than an oil based dressing, this can also be made with nonfat yogurt instead of cottage cheese.

Serves 8

2 cups low fat cottage cheese
4 tablespoons fresh herbs, such as basil, or 4 tablespoons fresh parsley
5 scallions roughly chopped, both white and green parts
1 teaspoon salt
freshly ground black pepper
2 tablespoons fresh lemon juice
3/4 cup buttermilk
2 cloves of fresh garlic

Method

Put all ingredients into a blender and blend until smooth. Use slightly more or less liquid depending on desired thickness.

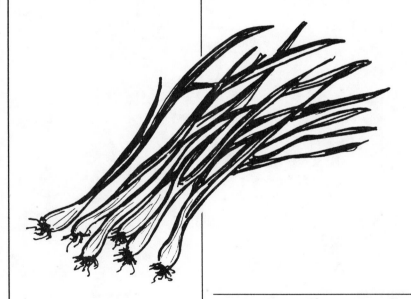

Nutrient Values:

Calories:	69.8	Cholesterol:	5.59 mg
Protein:	8.85 g	Fiber:	0.394 g
Carbohydrates:	5.25 g	% Fat Calories:	18
Total Fat:	1.36 g		

Curry Mustard Dressing

If you prefer a smoother, creamier dressing, try making this with nonfat yogurt instead of cottage cheese.

Serves 12

2 cups low fat cottage cheese
1 cup nonfat dry milk
1/3 cup Dijon mustard
1 teaspoon curry powder

Method

Put all ingredients in a blender or food processor, blend until smooth. Serve immediately.

Nutrient Values:

Calories:	60.2	Cholesterol:	4.17 mg
Protein:	7.52 g	Fiber:	0.086 g
Carbohydrates:	4.87 g	% Fat Calories:	17
Total Fat:	1.10 g		

Garlic Basil Dressing

This low fat dressing is excellent when you use fresh basil. Do not try to substitute dried.

Serves 4

1 cup nonfat yogurt
1/3 cup fresh basil
2 tablespoons 2% low fat cottage cheese
1 tablespoon chopped fresh parsley
1 tablespoon lemon juice
1 teaspoon Dijon mustard
1 teaspoon fresh garlic, crushed
salt and freshly ground black pepper

Method

Blend in a food processor or blender until smooth. Serve at once.

Nutrient Values:

Calories:	46.1	Cholesterol:	1.59 mg
Protein:	4.64 g	Fiber:	0.416 g
Carbohydrates:	6.47 g	% Fat Calories:	7
Total Fat:	0.388 g		

Thousand Island Dressing

Notice the difference in percent fat calories when you use mayonnaise to make this dressing!

Serves 4

1 cup nonfat yogurt
1/4 cup low calorie ketchup
2 tablespoons minced dill pickle
2 tablespoons 2% low fat cottage cheese,
    or 2 teaspoons low calorie mayonnaise
1 teaspoon horseradish
1 teaspoon Dijon mustard
salt and pepper

Method

Combine all ingredients in a bowl and mix well.

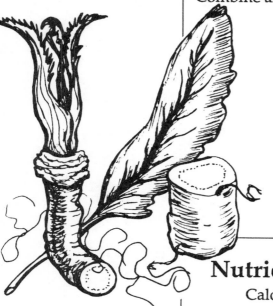

Nutrient Values: *(with mayonnaise)*

Calories:	69.4	Cholesterol:	2.81 mg
Protein:	3.72 g	Fiber:	0.395 g
Carbohydrates:	10.2 g	% Fat Calories:	21
Total Fat:	1.68 g		

Nutrient Values: *(with cottage cheese)*

Calories:	58.4	Cholesterol:	1.59 mg
Protein:	4.67 g	Fiber:	0.395 g
Carbohydrates:	9.29 g	% Fat Calories:	6
Total Fat:	0.379 g		

Dill Sauce with Dijon Mustard

This sauce is good served with either hot or cold fish dishes, and can also be used as a salad dressing.

Serves 4

1/2 cup nonfat yogurt
1/2 cup low fat cottage cheese
3 tablespoons chopped fresh dill, or 3 tablespoons chopped fresh parsley and 1 1/2 teaspoons dried dillweed
2 1/4 teaspoons Dijon style mustard

Method

Combine all ingredients in a blender or food processor, and process until smooth. Serve immediately.

Nutrient Values:

Calories:	44.6	Cholesterol:	2.88 mg
Protein:	5.71 g	Fiber:	0.165 g
Carbohydrates:	3.58 g	% Fat Calories:	15
Total Fat:	0.733 g		

Yogurt Cheese

This is a great substitute for cream cheese, and is used in the vegetable lasagna, and blintz recipes. Use it also as a base for dips — it is only 3% fat compared to regular cream cheese which is 90% fat, and has almost 75% less sodium.

Not all yogurts separate well, namely those that contain stabilizers or gelatin.

Makes 10 ounces

2 pounds plain nonfat yogurt

Method

Line a colander or sieve with a double layer of cheesecloth, and place over a bowl. Allow the cheesecloth to extend well over the outside edges of the colander. Stir the yogurt until it is well blended, and then pour it into the colander, folding over the edges of the cheesecloth to cover the yogurt. Refrigerate, and allow to drain overnight. Remove the yogurt from the cheesecloth, and discard the liquid in the bowl.

Variations: Add honey or sugar to desired sweetness, and/or pieces of dried fruit or raisins.

Nutrient Values: *(2 tablespoons)*

Calories:	25.4	Cholesterol:	0.799 mg
Protein:	2.60 g	Fiber:	0 g
Carbohydrates:	3.48 g	% Fat Calories:	3
Total Fat:	0.082 g		

Mock Sour Cream

This is a good base for many low fat dips. If you are watching your sodium intake, use the dry-curd cottage cheese, since it is much lower in sodium.

Makes over 1 cup

1 cup low fat cottage cheese
3 tablespoons plain nonfat yogurt

Method

Puree ingredients in blender or food processor until smooth.

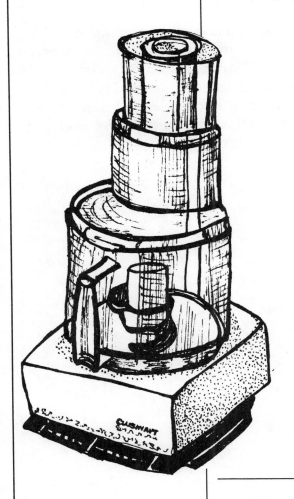

Nutrient Values:

Calories:	14.3	Cholesterol:	1.23 mg
Protein:	2.10 g	Fiber:	0 g
Carbohydrates:	0.716 g	% Fat Calories:	18
Total Fat:	0.277 g		

Low Fat Pesto

Pesto is traditionally made with olive oil, and is very high in fat. Try this as a substitute.

Serves 6

1/4 cup chicken stock
1 cup fresh basil
3 tablespoons freshly grated Parmesan cheese
3 cloves garlic
salt and pepper to taste

Method

Bring the chicken broth to boiling in a small saucepan. Set aside. Meanwhile, combine the basil, Parmesan, and garlic, in a blender or food processor. Process until chopped, about 30 seconds. With the motor running, pour the broth through the feed tube of the blender or food processor, and continue to blend until mixture is a smooth paste. Season to taste with salt and pepper. Cover and refrigerate for several hours before using.

Nutrient Values:

Calories:	26.4	Cholesterol:	2.01 mg
Protein:	2.00 g	Fiber:	0.825 g
Carbohydrates:	3.37 g	% Fat Calories:	30
Total Fat:	1.01 g		

To Thicken Sauces and Gravies:
Flour and other powdered starches expand when they are dissolved in liquid and heated, and this is the reason they are used as thickeners.

Arrowroot and cornstarch will thicken a mixture without making it cloudy. Use 1 tablespoon in a little cold water, mixed to a smooth paste, to thicken 1 cup of hot liquid to the consistency of a medium sauce. You can also use twice the amount of flour to achieve the same results, but the sauce will be cloudy.

Sweet and Sour Sauce

This delicious sweet and sour sauce can be used with roast pork, or poultry. It is low in both fat and calories!

Serves 6

1/2 cup pineapple juice
2 tablespoons lemon juice
1 tablespoon white vinegar
2 tablespoons brown sugar
1 tablespoon low sodium soy sauce
1 tablespoon cornstarch
1/4 teaspoon powdered ginger
1/4 green pepper
1 can (9 ounces) pineapple tidbits, undrained

Method

Combine all of the ingredients except for the can of undrained pineapple tidbits in a blender or food processor. Blend until all ingredients are mixed. The peppers should be chopped moderately fine. Do not puree the peppers. Pour the mixture into a saucepan and add the undrained pineapple tidbits. Cook over moderate heat for several minutes or until thick and clear.

Nutrient Values:

Calories:	53.5	Cholesterol:	0 mg
Protein:	0.404 g	Fiber:	0.518 g
Carbohydrates:	13.7 g	% Fat Calories:	1
Total Fat:	0.518 g		

Cumberland Sauce

This sauce is delicious with ham, chicken or turkey. It can also be used as a glaze.

Serves 5-6

3/4 cup currant jelly
1/4 cup frozen orange juice concentrate
2 teaspoons Dijon style mustard
1/4 teaspoon ground ginger
2-3 dashes hot red pepper sauce
2-4 tablespoons port wine

Method

Heat all ingredients in a small saucepan, and bring to a boil.
Lower heat and simmer for 1 minute.

Nutrient Values:

Calories:	163	Cholesterol:	0 mg
Protein:	0.754 g	Fiber:	0.626 g
Carbohydrates:	39.4 g	% Fat Calories:	1
Total Fat:	0.174 g		

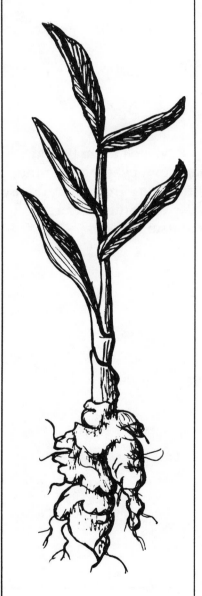

Ginger Whipped Cream

This is a good substitute for whipped cream if you enjoy the flavor of ginger. Serve with ginger muffins.

Serves 8

1/3 cup partially frozen ice water
2/3 cup nonfat milk powder
1 teaspoon powdered ginger
2 tablespoons powdered sugar or equivalent sweetener (optional)

Method

In a chilled bowl with chilled beaters, beat together partially frozen ice water with milk powder and powdered ginger for 5 minutes on high speed of electric mixer. Mixture will become very thick, just like whipping cream. Add the sugar if using, and mix well. Use immediately.

Nutrient Values:

Calories:	33.8	Cholesterol:	1.03 mg
Protein:	2.07 g	Fiber:	0.013 g
Carbohydrates:	6.32 g	% Fat Calories:	2
Total Fat:	0.057 g		

Whipped Cream Topping

This is a good substitute for whipped cream, and will keep for one day refrigerated.

Makes 4 cups

1 1/2 teaspoons unflavored gelatin
1/4 cup boiling water
2 tablespoons sugar
1 cup ice water
1/2 cup instant nonfat dry milk
1 tablespoon vanilla extract

Method

Chill the bowl and the beaters well. Dissolve gelatin in boiling water and stir in the sugar. In the chilled bowl beat together the ice water, nonfat dry milk and vanilla until very frothy. Gradually add the gelatin mixture. Continue beating until the mixture is quite stiff. Chill for at least 1 hour before using. Keeps 1 day refrigerated.

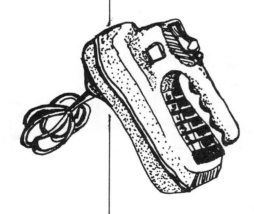

Nutrient Values: *(2 tablespoons)*

Calories:	7.60	Cholesterol:	0.188 mg
Protein:	0.561 g	Fiber:	0.031 g
Carbohydrates:	1.33 g	% Fat Calories:	1
Total Fat:	0.008 g		

Creamy Whipped Cream

This substitute whipped cream has to be used immediately or it begins to break down into liquid again. Be sure the bowl and beaters are well chilled before you begin.

Makes 6 cups

1-20 ounce can evaporated skim milk, chilled
3 tablespoons sugar
1 tablespoon vanilla extract

Method

In a large chilled bowl with chilled beaters, beat the evaporated skim milk until foamy. Add the sugar and vanilla and continue to beat until the mixture is the consistency of whipped cream. Use at once.

Nutrient Values: *(2 tablespoons)*

Calories:	12.3	Cholesterol:	0.463 mg
Protein:	0.880 g	Fiber:	0 g
Carbohydrates:	2.12 g	% Fat Calories:	2
Total Fat:	0.024 g		

Blueberry Sauce

Spoon this sauce over frozen yogurt, angel food cake, or assorted fresh fruit.

Makes 6 servings - 1/4 cup each

2 cups fresh or frozen blueberries
1/4 cup sugar
1 tablespoon fresh lemon juice
1/2 teaspoon vanilla

Method

Mix together all ingredients in a heavy bottomed saucepan. Bring to boil, and boil for 1-2 minutes stirring constantly. Add vanilla. Store in the refrigerator, covered. Serve as desired.

Nutrient Values:

Calories:	60.0	Cholesterol:	0 mg
Protein:	0.33 g	Fiber:	1.31 g
Carbohydrates:	15.3 g	% Fat Calories:	3
Total Fat:	0.191 g		

Raspberry Topping

This topping is good over pound cake, angel food cake or frozen yogurt.

Makes 1 1/2 cups

1 pint fresh or frozen raspberries
2 tablespoons sugar
1 teaspoon cornstarch
1/4 teaspoon cinnamon

Method

Combine all ingredients in a small saucepan. Cook and stir for 2 minutes over low heat. Cool before serving.

Nutrient Values:

Calories:	47.5	Cholesterol:	0 mg
Protein:	0.266 g	Fiber:	1.75 g
Carbohydrates:	12.2 g	% Fat Calories:	1
Total Fat:	0.062 g		

Strawberry Framboise Sauce

This delicious sauce is good over frozen yogurt, blintzes or pancakes.

Makes 1 cup

1 package frozen, sweetened strawberries (10 ounces) thawed, drained, juice reserved
1 teaspoon arrowroot or cornstarch
3 tablespoons framboise or other strawberry liqueur (optional)

Method

Blend reserved juice and the arrowroot or cornstarch in a small pan. Heat to boiling stirring constantly. Boil 1 minute. Remove from heat and stir in the strawberries and framboise. Puree in a blender or food processor.

Nutrient Values: *(2 tablespoons)*

Calories:	58.5	Cholesterol:	0 mg
Protein:	0.190 g	Fiber:	1.06 g
Carbohydrates:	12.2 g	% Fat Calories:	1
Total Fat:	0.062 g		

Apple, Date and Raisin Chutney

This delicious chutney is good with roast chicken or turkey, cold cuts, and salads.

Makes over 2 pounds of chutney

1 pound cooking apples, coarsely grated
3 medium sized onions, coarsely grated
1 large green pepper, finely chopped
1 large red pepper, finely chopped
1/2 cup pitted dates, finely chopped
1 cup dark raisins
2 tablespoons chopped crystallized ginger, finely chopped
2 tablespoons white wine vinegar
1/2 teaspoon salt
1 tablespoon sugar
1/4 cup lemon juice
1 teaspoon cinnamon
1 teaspoon powdered ginger
1/4 teaspoon cloves
1/4 teaspoon mace
1/4 teaspoon coriander

Method

In a large mixing bowl mix together all ingredients except the vinegar, salt, sugar, lemon juice and spices. Blend ingredients together well.

In a small bowl stir together vinegar, salt, sugar, and lemon juice. Pour over the chopped fruit mixture and mix well. Mix together all spices in a small bowl and stir into the mixture.

Place mixture into a large non-stick pot, and cook over medium heat until onions and apples are tender — about 30 minutes. Cool and refrigerate for several hours or overnight before using.

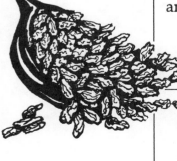

Nutrient Values:

Calories:	40.1	Cholesterol:	0 mg
Protein:	0.483 g	Fiber:	1.23 g
Carbohydrates:	10.4 g	% Fat Calories:	3
Total Fat:	0.165 g		

Beverages

These delicious, low fat beverages, are a wonderful way to start the day, or can be used as a refreshing drink anytime. Both children and adults will enjoy these - many of these drinks taste like high fat milk shakes!

Your Notes:

Beverages

Your Notes:

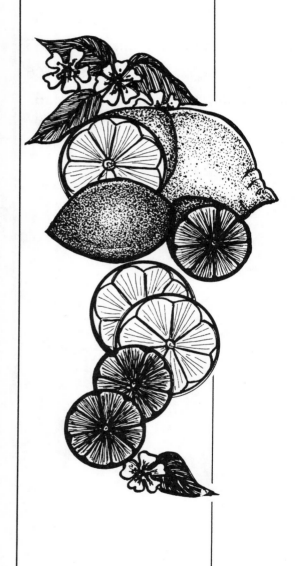

Strawberry Yogurt Drink

This is probably my favorite breakfast drink — it tastes just like a milkshake! Of course you can drink it anytime of the day or night, and children really love it also.

Serves 2

1 cup fresh strawberries
3 teaspoons lemon juice
4 tablespoons sugar
1/2 teaspoon vanilla
1 cup low fat plain yogurt
1 cup 2% low fat milk

Method

Blend all ingredients in a blender until well mixed. Serve immediately.

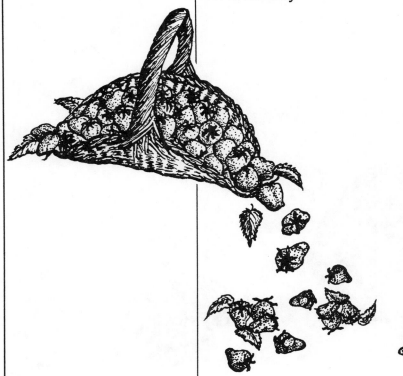

Nutrient Values:

Calories:	245	Cholesterol:	13.0 mg
Protein:	11.0 g	Fiber:	1.96 g
Carbohydrates:	45.3 g	% Fat Calories:	10
Total Fat:	2.89 g		

Blackberry Apple Spritzer

This refreshing drink is a good source of vitamin C and fiber. It is an excellent substitute for sodas.

Serves 4

2 cups apple juice
1-12 ounce package frozen blackberries
1 tablespoon honey or sugar
2 cups seltzer sparkling water, blackberry flavored if possible

Method

In a blender or food processor combine the apple juice and honey or sugar. Blend until smooth. Add the carbonated water slowly, stirring gently to mix. Serve over ice cubes.

Nutrient Values:

Calories:	126	Cholesterol:	0 mg
Protein:	1.19 g	Fiber:	4.48 g
Carbohydrates:	31.5 g	% Fat Calories:	3
Total Fat:	0.491 g		

Grapefruit Spritzer

This is a refreshing drink that is expecially good in the summertime. Serve with lots of ice.

Serves 4

1 can unsweetened, frozen grapefruit juice concentrate
3 cups club soda, or grapefruit flavored seltzer

Method

Mix together frozen juice concentrate adding 3 cups of club soda or grapefruit flavored seltzer instead of water. Serve in tall glasses with ice cubes.

Variations: Orange juice, pineapple juice, and cranberry juice, are all very good made this way.

Nutrient Values:

Calories:	123	Cholesterol:	0 mg
Protein:	1.64 g	Fiber:	1.15 g
Carbohydrates:	29.6 g	% Fat Calories:	3
Total Fat:	0.411 g		

Peachy Orange Shake

You can use drained, canned, unsweetened peaches, if fresh ones are not available.

Serves 2

2 medium sized fresh peaches, unpeeled and sliced
juice of 1 fresh lime
1 1/2 cups fresh orange juice
1/4 cup crushed ice

Method

Puree peaches in a blender or food processor. Add remaining ingredients and blend at high speed.

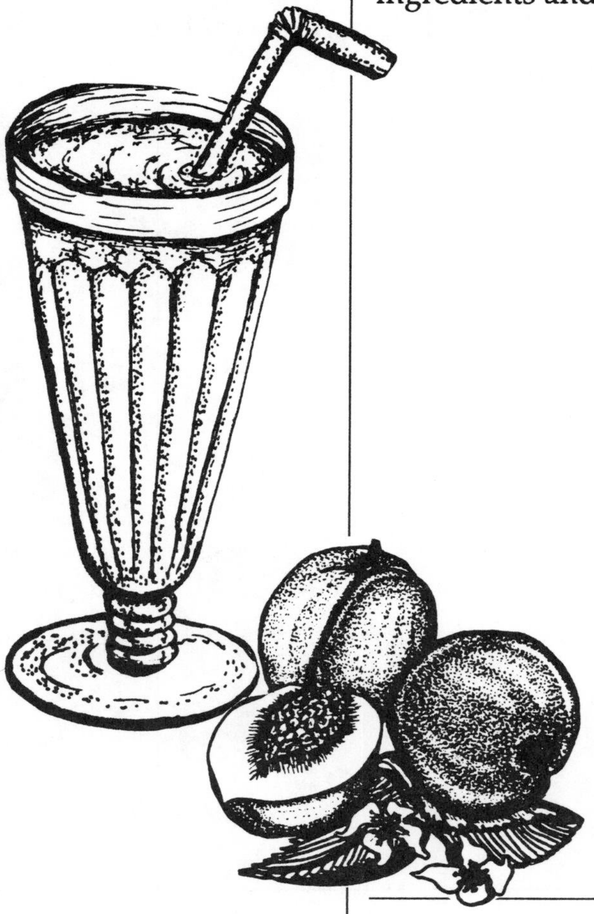

Nutrient Values:

Calories:	124	Cholesterol:	0 mg
Protein:	1.94 g	Fiber:	1.94 g
Carbohydrates:	31.1 g	% Fat Calories:	1
Total Fat:	0.201 g		

Fresh Peach Shake

This is a great drink to have before your morning exercise!

Serves 2

2 cups fresh peaches, unpeeled and sliced
3/4 cup cold water
3 tablespoons fresh lime juice
3 tablespoons sugar or honey
3 tablespoons nonfat dry milk
1 tablespoon wheat germ (optional)
pinch salt

Method

Combine all ingredients in a blender or food processor, and blend for 1 minute. Serve at once over crushed ice.

Nutrient Values:

Calories:	1 3 8	Cholesterol:	1.13 mg
Protein:	3.62 g	Fiber:	1.94 g
Carbohydrates:	33.5 g	% Fat Calories:	3
Total Fat:	0.449 g		

Banana Shake

This delicious creamy shake is good for breakfast, and also makes a delicious snack.

Serves 2

1 cup banana or plain nonfat yogurt
1 cup apple juice
1 large banana, sliced, wrapped in foil and frozen
2 egg whites
1 teaspoon vanilla
2 or 3 ice cubes

Method

In a blender or food processor combine all of the ingredients except the ice cubes. Cover and blend until smooth. Add the ice cubes one at a time, blending until smooth after each addition.

Nutrient Values:

Calories:	93.8	Cholesterol:	1.00 mg
Protein:	5.30 g	Fiber:	0.630 g
Carbohydrates:	18.15 g	% Fat Calories:	3
Total Fat:	0.302 g		

Tropical Shake

This drink is good served as a fast breakfast, or as a nourishing refreshment on a hot summer day.

Serves 2

8 ounces fresh pineapple, cut into chunks, or 1-8 ounce can unsweetened pineapple, drained
1 medium sized banana
1 cup plain nonfat yogurt

Method

Place all ingredients in a blender or food processor, and blend for 30 seconds. Serve immediately.

Nutrient Values:

Calories:	172	Cholesterol:	2.00 mg
Protein:	7.53 g	Fiber:	2.82 g
Carbohydrates:	36.1 g	% Fat Calories:	5
Total Fat:	0.960 g		

Orange Milk Shake

Here is another "breakfast on the run", or serve as a low fat snack or beverage.

Serves 1

1 cup unsweetened orange juice
1/4 cup instant nonfat dry milk
1/4 teaspoon pure vanilla extract

Method

Place all ingredients in a blender or food processor, and blend for 30 seconds. Serve immediately.

Nutrient Values:

Calories:	172	Cholesterol:	3.00 mg
Protein:	7.71 g	Fiber:	0.992 g
Carbohydrates:	34.7 g	% Fat Calories:	3
Total Fat:	0.627 g		

Tomato-Yogurt Drink

This can be served as a non-alcoholic cocktail, or as a breakfast drink.

Serves 1

1 cup tomato juice
1 1/2 teaspoons lemon juice
1/4 teaspoon grated fresh ginger
1 cup nonfat yogurt

Method

Place all ingredients in a food processor or blender, and blend for 30 seconds. Serve immediately.

Nutrient Values:

Calories:	170	Cholesterol:	4.00 mg
Protein:	14.9 g	Fiber:	1.93 g
Carbohydrates:	28.4 g	% Fat Calories:	3
Total Fat:	0.576 g		

Apricot Smoothie

If you do not wish to use dry apricots, substitute unsweetened, canned apricots, and use the reserved juice instead of the water called for in the recipe. Apricots are a good source of vitamin A. According to the American Cancer Society, this vitamin may be an agent that can reduce the tendency for malignant cells to multiply.

Serves 4

1 pound dried apricots, soaked
2 cups water in which apricots were soaked
2 cups 2% low fat milk
4 drops pure vanilla extract

Method

Blend all ingredients in a blender or food processor until smooth. Serve at once.

Nutrient Values:

Calories:	132	Cholesterol:	11.0 mg
Protein:	4.67 g	Fiber:	1.28 g
Carbohydrates:	24.5 g	% Fat Calories:	16
Total Fat:	2.44 g		

Party Punch

This is a good non-alcoholic drink to make for a crowd. The recipe can be halved or doubled.

Serves 14

2 pints sweet cider
1 cup fresh orange juice
1/4 cup fresh lemon juice
2 cups unsweetened pineapple juice
1 cup unsweetened cranberry juice
pinch ground cloves
1 banana, thinly sliced
1 large fresh pineapple, peeled, cored, and cut into small chunks

Method

Place all liquids in a punch bowl, and stir well to blend. Sprinkle with the ground cloves. Float banana slices, and pineapple chunks in the punch.

Nutrient Values:

Calories:	93.1	Cholesterol:	0 mg
Protein:	0.510 g	Fiber:	0.967 g
Carbohydrates:	23.2 g	% Fat Calories:	3
Total Fat:	0.336 g		

Breads and Muffins

Nothing surpasses the wonderful aroma of freshly baked breads and muffins, and nothing tastes better either. These breads and muffins are quick, and easy to prepare, are low in fat, (as long as you don't spread on extra butter) and a good source of fiber, vitamins and minerals. Bake them fresh for breakfast, or make them part of any meal. They make great nutritious snacks, can be taken on picnics, or packed in lunches. Enjoy them, but remember that as with all items containing sugar, they should be eaten in moderation.

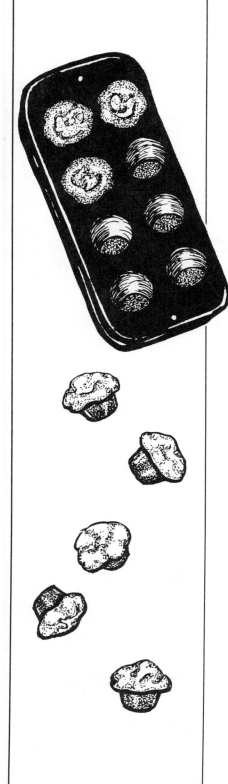

Breads and Muffins

Banana Whole Wheat Bread

This plain banana bread is very flavorful, and is good as a breakfast bread or a snack. Be sure to use very ripe bananas.

Makes 16 slices

1 cup all-purpose flour
3/4 cup whole wheat flour
1 teaspoon baking soda
1/4 teaspoon salt
1/2 cup sugar
1/4 cup vegetable oil
2 egg whites
1 cup mashed ripe bananas (about 2 medium)
1 teaspoon vanilla extract

Method

Pre-heat the oven to 350 degrees and place the oven rack in the center of the oven.

Combine flours, baking soda, and salt in a bowl, and set aside. In the bowl of a food processor mix together the sugar, oil, egg whites, bananas, and vanilla, and beat until thick and creamy, about 1 minute. Add the flour mixture, just until blended.

Pour the batter into an 8x4x2-inch loaf pan coated with cooking spray. Bake for 45 minutes, or until a wooden toothpick inserted in the center comes out clean. Remove from oven and let stand on a wire rack for 10 minutes. Remove from pan, and let cool completely on the wire rack before cutting.

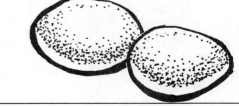

Nutrient Values

Calories:	121	Cholesterol:	0 mg
Protein:	2.15 g	Fiber:	1.33 g
Carbohydrates:	20.7 g	% Fat Calories:	27
Total Fat:	3.69 g		

Blueberry Tea Loaf

Mix up this quick and easy recipe for breakfast, lunch, dinner, or a snack. Frozen blueberries may be used instead of fresh ones if you like.

Makes 16 slices

1 cup all-purpose flour
1 cup whole wheat pastry flour
1 cup sugar
3 teaspoons baking powder
1/4 teaspoon salt
1 1/2 cups blueberries, rinsed well and patted dry
1 egg
2 egg whites
1 cup skim or low fat milk
3 tablespoons safflower oil
1 teaspoon grated fresh orange peel
confectioner's sugar

Method

Preheat oven to 350 degrees. Lightly spray a 9 x 5 x 3-inch non-stick loaf pan, and set aside.

In a large bowl, mix together both flours, sugar, baking powder, and salt. Gently fold in the blueberries.

Beat together egg, egg whites, milk, oil and orange peel; add all at once to flour mixture. Stir just until dry ingredients are moistened.

Bake for 50-60 minutes or until a toothpick inserted in the center comes out clean. Remove from the oven and cool in the pan on a wire rack for 10 minutes. Turn loaf out of pan and allow to completely cool before cutting. Sprinkle with confectioners sugar before cutting to serve.

Nutrient Values:

Calories:	142	Cholesterol:	17.4 mg
Protein:	3.14 g	Fiber:	1.47 g
Carbohydrates:	26.0 g	% Fat Calories:	20
Total Fat:	3.25 g		

Banana and Apple Loaf

This delicious loaf contains no added fat and yet is very moist and tasty. It is excellent eaten plain, or as an accompaniment with chicken salad. I have had trouble keeping it for more than a couple of days; it is always eaten very quckly!

Makes 20 slices

2 eggs
2 very ripe medium sized bananas
1 teaspoon pure vanilla extract
1/2 cup sugar
2 cups whole wheat pastry flour
2 teaspoons apple pie spice
1 teaspoon baking soda
2 teaspoons double-acting baking powder
1/2 teaspoon salt
1/2 cup raisins
2 medium sized apples, unpeeled, cored and chopped

Method

Preheat oven to 350 degrees.

In a food processor or electric mixer, beat together the eggs, bananas, vanilla, and sugar. Sift together flour, apple pie spice, baking powder, baking soda, and salt; add to banana mixture being careful not to overmix. Fold in the raisins and apples. Spoon into nonstick loaf pan lightly sprayed with cooking spray.

Bake in preheated 350 degree oven 40-50 minutes. Loaf is done when a toothpick inserted into the center comes out clean.

Remove pan to a wire rack and let cool for 10-15 minutes before turning it out onto the rack. Cool completely before cutting; it will still continue to cook as it cools.

Nutrient Values

Calories:	104	Cholesterol:	27.4 mg
Protein:	2.51 g	Fiber:	2.56 g
Carbohydrates:	23.0 g	% Fat Calories:	8
Total Fat:	.954 g		

<u>No Buttermilk or Sour Milk:</u>
Use yogurt or use 1 tablespoon lemon juice or vinegar, plus enough milk to make 1 cup; let stand 5 minutes before using.

Whole Wheat Irish Soda Bread with Raisins

The bread can be mixed together in a few minutes, and is good for breakfast, lunch, or dinner.

Makes 16 slices

2 cups whole wheat flour
2 cups all-purpose flour
2 tablespoons granulated sugar
2 teaspoons baking powder
1 1/2 teaspoons baking soda
1 teaspoon salt
2 tablespoons butter
1 cup dark raisins
1 3/4 cups buttermilk (or 1 3/4 cups 2% low fat milk, plus 2 tablespoons vinegar)

Method

Preheat oven to 350° degrees.

Combine flours, sugar, baking powder, baking soda, and salt, in a food processor or bowl. Cut in the butter - using a pastry blender if doing it by hand, until the mixture is crumbly. Add the the raisins, and stir to mix; add buttermilk, and mix to form soft dough. Remove from bowl, and knead about 8 times, or until dough is smooth.

Place the dough on a greased baking sheet; flatten into a circle about 2 1/2 inches thick, and cut an x about 1/4 inch deep on top.

Bake for 1 hour, or until toothpick inserted in the center comes out clean. Cool on a wire rack.

Nutrient Values:

Calories:	168	Cholesterol:	4.87 mg
Protein:	4.87 g	Fiber:	2.91 g
Carbohydrates:	33.7 g	% Fat Calories:	11
Total Fat:	2.18 g		

Honey or molasses is easier to measure and will pour out more easily if you lightly spray the inside of the measuring cup with cooking spray, or coat it lightly with oil.

Spicy Gingerbread Muffins

These light and spicy muffins are delicious plain or can be "dressed up" and served with ginger whipped cream (p. 45), or low fat yogurt.

Makes 16 muffins

1 cup whole wheat pastry flour
1 teaspoon baking soda
1/4 teaspoon salt
1/4 teaspoon ground black pepper
1 teaspoon ground ginger
1/2 teaspoon ground cloves
1/2 teaspoon cinnamon
1/4 teaspoon dry mustard powder
2 bananas, not too ripe, and well mashed if using an electric mixer
1/2 cup sugar
1/2 cup molasses
1/4 cup oil

Method

Preheat oven to 375 degrees. Lightly spray non-stick cupcake forms, or line them with papers.

Sift together flour, baking soda, salt, pepper, ginger, cloves, cinnamon, and mustard and set aside. In a food processor or electric mixer, beat bananas until very light, about 1 minute in a food processor, or 2-3 minutes with an electric mixer. Add sugar, oil, and molasses, and continue to beat until well mixed. Add the sifted dry ingredients, and mix only until just incorporated.

Bake for 18-20 minutes or until tops spring back when gently pressed with fingertip. Be sure not to overbake, so begin to test after 15 minutes. Cool on a wire rack.

Nutrient Values:

Calories:	114	Cholesterol:	0 mg
Protein:	1.16 g	Fiber:	1.26 g
Carbohydrates:	20.6 g	% Fat Calories:	27
Total Fat:	3.65 g		

To eliminate muffins from sticking to the pan:
Place the hot pan on a wet towel. The muffins will slide right out.

Banana-Raisin Muffins

Never refrigerate bananas. If you buy them yellow and firm, they will ripen quite quickly at room temperature. The riper they become, the more intense the flavor.

Makes 16 muffins.

1 cup all-purpose flour
1 cup whole wheat pastry flour
1 tablespoon wheat germ
1 tablespoon oat bran
2 tablespoons double-acting baking powder
1 teaspoon ground cinnamon
1/2 teaspoon salt
1/4 cup oil
1/2 cup granulated sugar
1 egg
1 teaspoon vanilla extract
3 medium bananas, peeled and mashed
1 cup dark raisins

Method

Preheat oven to 400 degrees. Sift together flour, baking powder, cinnamon, wheat germ, bran, and salt. Set aside.

In a food processor or electric mixer combine oil, sugar, egg, vanilla, and bananas, and beat until light and fluffy. Add the flour mixture and mix until just moistened. Fold in the raisins.

Place muffin papers in the muffin pan. Fill each paper 2/3 full. Bake for 15 - 20 minutes or until muffins are lightly browned and a toothpick, inserted in the center comes out dry.

Remove muffins to a wire rack and cool.

Nutrient Values:

Calories:	162	Cholesterol:	0 mg
Protein:	2.84 g	Fiber:	2.31 g
Carbohydrates:	31.0 g	% Fat Calories:	20
Total Fat:	3.82 g		

Blueberry Muffins

Try these delicious, unusual muffins. Blueberries provide vitamins A and C, potassium, calcium, iron, and manganese.

Makes 20 muffins

1 1/4 cups whole wheat pastry flour
1 1/4 cups all purpose flour
1 tablespoon baking powder
1/2 teaspoon baking soda
1/2 teaspoon salt
1/3 cup sugar
1 teaspoon cinnamon
1/2 teaspoon ginger
1 egg
1 cup buttermilk
1/4 cup safflower oil
1/2 cup dark molasses
1 cup blueberries (rinsed well and patted dry, if they are frozen)

Method

Preheat oven to 400 degrees. Stir together flour, baking powder, baking soda, salt, sugar, cinnamon, and ginger. Mix egg, buttermilk, oil, and molasses together well. Add this mixture to the dry ingredients. Stir only until just moistened. Fold in the blueberries very gently.

Line muffin pans with paper liners, and fill each paper 2/3 full. Bake for 15-20 minutes, or until done. Cool on a wire rack.

Nutrient Values:

Calories:	120	Cholesterol:	14.1 mg
Protein:	2.59 g	Fiber:	1.56 g
Carbohydrates:	20.7 g	% Fat Calories:	25
Total Fat:	3.39 g		

Oatmeal and Raisin Muffins

Makes 14 muffins

1 cup whole wheat pastry flour
2 teaspoons double-acting baking powder
1 teaspoon cinnamon
1/4 teaspoon salt
4 1/2 ounces quick or old-fashioned oats
1 cup dark raisins
1/4 cup vegetable oil
6 tablespoons brown sugar
1 teaspoon vanilla
2 eggs
1 cup low fat milk

Method

Preheat oven to 375 degrees. Line 12 muffin-pan cups with paper baking cups.

In a small bowl stir together the flour, baking powder, cinnamon, salt, oats, and raisins; set aside. In a medium electric mixing bowl mix together oil, sugar, and vanilla. Add the milk and eggs, and mix together well. Combine this mixture with the dry ingredients, and stir only until just moistened.

Fill each cup with an equal amount of batter (about 2/3 full), and bake for 20 to 25 minutes. Muffins will be lightly browned, and a toothpick inserted in center comes out dry.

Remove muffins to wire rack to cool.

Nutrient Values:

Calories:	152	Cholesterol:	39.9 mg
Protein:	3.59 g	Fiber:	2.17 g
Carbohydrates:	24.5 g	% Fat Calories:	30
Total Fat:	5.31 g		

Apple Raisin Muffins

Makes 16 muffins

1 cup all-purpose flour
1 cup whole wheat pastry flour
2 tablespoons double-acting baking powder
2 teaspoons apple pie spice
1/2 teaspoon salt
1 cup dark raisins
1/2 cup granulated sugar
1/4 cup safflower oil
1 banana, not too ripe
1 egg white
1 teaspoon vanilla extract
1 cup applesauce

Method

Preheat oven to 400 degrees. Sift together the flours, baking powder, apple pie spice, and salt. Stir in the raisins and set aside.

In a food processor or electric mixer combine the sugar, oil, banana, egg white, and vanilla, and beat until light and fluffy. Add the applesauce, and mix into the batter. Stir this mixture into the dry ingredients until just moistened.

Fill paper-lined muffin pans 2/3 full, and bake for 15 - 20 minutes or until lightly browned, and a toothpick inserted into the muffin, comes out clean. Cool on a wire rack.

Nutrient Values:

Calories:	154	Cholesterol:	0 mg
Protein:	2.62 g	Fiber:	2.21 g
Carbohydrates:	29.2 g	% Fat Calories:	21
Total Fat:	3.73 g		

Pumpkin Raisin Muffins

These delicious muffins are a good source of fiber, and unlike most muffins, will keep well for several days.

Makes 12 muffins

1 1/4 cups whole wheat blend flour
1/4 cup oat bran
3/4 cup granulated sugar
1 1/2 teaspoons cinnamon
1 teaspoon baking powder
1 teaspoon baking soda
1/2 teaspoon salt
1 cup raisins
1 cup mashed or canned cooked pumpkin
2 large eggs
1/4 cup safflower oil
2/3 cup nonfat yogurt

Method

Preheat oven to 400 degrees.

In a large bowl, combine flour, bran, sugar, cinnamon, baking powder, baking soda, salt, and raisins. Stir well to mix. Add pumpkin, eggs, oil, and yogurt; stir just to combine.

Spoon the batter into paper-lined or non-stick muffin tins, and bake in the oven for 25 minutes or until tops spring back when lightly pressed. Cool on a wire rack.

Nutrient Values:

Calories:	204	Cholesterol:	45.9 mg
Protein:	4.05 g	Fiber:	2.53 g
Carbohydrates:	36.2 g	% Fat Calories:	25
Total Fat:	5.85 g		

Appetizers, Dips and Snacks

These low fat appetizers, dips and snacks will help you to lose weight, and are quick, and easy to prepare. Use crudites, (raw vegetables) instead of potato chips, for your dips, and arrange them attractively on platters or in baskets lined with lettuce leaves.

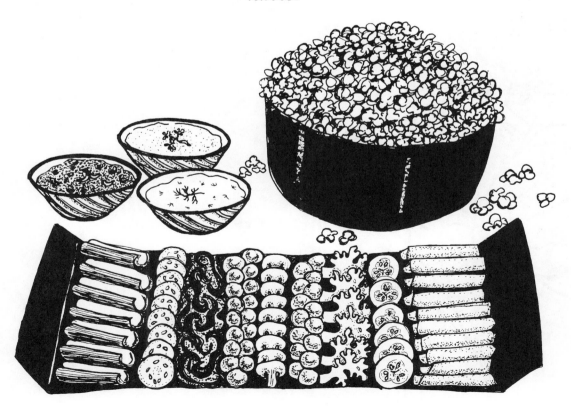

Appetizers, Dips and Snacks

Zucchini Stuffed with Crab

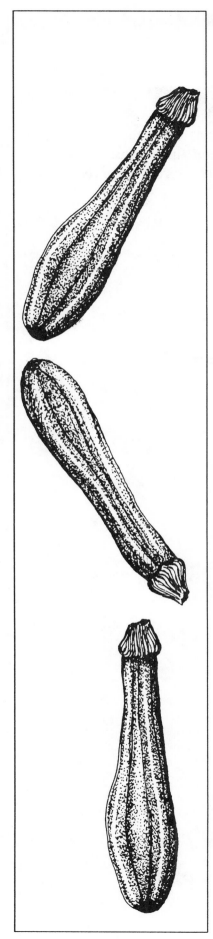

You can make this recipe substituting shrimp for the crabmeat, and it is equally delicious. Imitation crabmeat (which is pollack mixed with other ingredients) is available in most supermarkets, and in a recipe such as this one is a excellent substitute for the more expensive crabmeat, and is also very low in fat. This recipe can also be served for lunch, accompanied with a large tossed salad.

Serves 6

6 zucchini, trimmed, washed, and patted dry
2 teaspoons unsalted butter
1 medium sized onion, finely chopped
2 cloves garlic, minced
2 tablespoons all-purpose flour
2/3 cup clam juice, or dry white wine
8 ounces fresh, frozen, or imitation crabmeat,
       shredded into very fine flakes
1 tablespoon 2% low fat milk
1 1/2 teaspoons fresh lemon juice
1/4 teaspoon salt
freshly ground black pepper
1/4 cup fresh, whole wheat, or oatbran breadcrumbs
6 tablespoons freshly grated Parmesan cheese

Method

Preheat oven to 375 degrees. Lightly spray a large, shallow baking dish with cooking spray, and set aside.

Cut the zucchini in half lengthwise, and score the cut side lightly with the tines of a fork. Place the zucchini in the prepared baking dish, cut side down, and cover with foil. Bake 45-50 minutes or until they are cooked all the way through.

While the zucchini are baking prepare the stuffing as follows:

Melt the butter in a non-stick pan, and saute the onions and garlic for 4 minutes, or until soft but not brown. Stir the flour into the onions, and cook for one minute. Add the clam juice or wine, and bring the mixture to a boil, stirring constantly, until it becomes thick. Remove from the heat, and add the crabmeat, shrimp, lemon juice, salt and pepper.

Preheat the broiler.

When the zucchini are cooked, turn them over so that the cut sides are facing up. Divide the stuffing mixture evenly among the zucchini, smoothing the tops carefully.

Sprinkle the breadcrumbs evenly over the top of the stuffing, and place the dish under the broiler until the stuffing mixture is heated through, and the crumbs are golden brown. Serve hot.

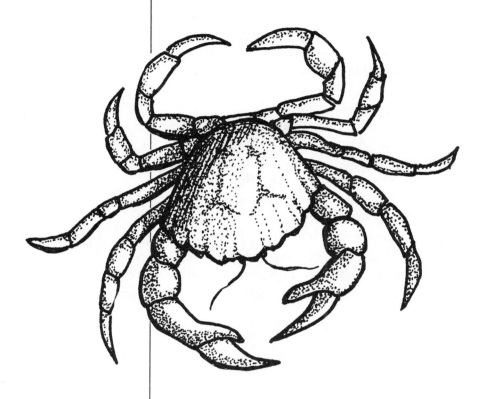

Nutrient Values:

Calories:	129	Cholesterol:	45.4 mg
Protein:	11.7 g	Fiber:	1.42 g
Carbohydrates:	8.23 g	% Fat Calories:	26
Total Fat:	3.81 g		

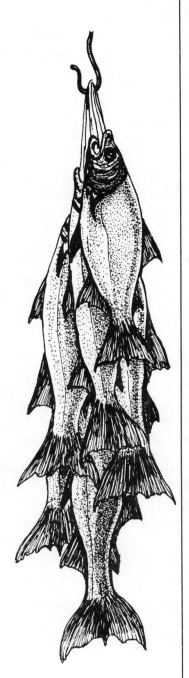

Rainbow Trout with Lemon-Yogurt Dressing

This salad is a good starter before a meal such as pasta primavera, or a vegetable stew.

Serves 6

1 1/2 pounds rainbow trout, cleaned, rinsed well and patted dry
5 tablespoons dry white wine

Dressing

3/4 cup plain nonfat yogurt
juice of half a lemon
1 tablespoon finely chopped fresh dill, or 1 tablespoon chopped fresh parsley
2 teaspoons virgin olive oil
salt and freshly ground black pepper

Salad

romaine lettuce
head lettuce
alfalfa sprouts
bean sprouts

Method

Preheat oven to 400 degrees.

Lay the fish on a piece of aluminum foil, and sprinkle with the wine. Enclose fish completely in the foil, and place in a shallow rectangular baking dish. Bake for 15 minutes. Carefully remove the fish from the foil, and allow to cool

Arrange the salad mixture on individual plates, and prepare the dressing by mixing all of the ingredients together in a small bowl.

Skin and fillet the cooled trout, and break into small pieces.

Drizzle the dressing over the salad, and arrange the trout on top. Serve immediately.

Nutrient Values:

Calories:	218	Cholesterol:	83.2 mg
Protein:	32.6 g	Fiber:	0.678 g
Carbohydrates:	3.82 g	% Fat Calories:	29
Total Fat:	6.58 g		

Marinated Mushrooms

These marinated mushrooms are much lower in fat than the traditional recipes. For maximum flavor allow them to marinate overnight.

Serves 8

3/4 cup dry white wine
juice from 1 large, fresh lemon
1 garlic clove, crushed
3/4 pound oyster mushrooms, trimmed, wiped, and sliced
3/4 pound fresh button mushrooms, trimmed, and wiped
2 teaspoons virgin olive oil
2 1/2 tablespoons fresh parsley
1/4 teaspoon salt
freshly ground black pepper
lettuce leaves

Method

Combine the wine, lemon juice, and garlic in a large saucepan, and bring the mixture to a boil. Reduce the heat, cover the pan, and gently simmer for 6-8 minutes, or until tender. Be careful not to overcook the mushrooms, they should still retain their shape.

Drain the mushrooms, reserving the liquid, and return the liquid to the saucepan. Reduce the liquid to about 1/2 cup, and remove from the heat. Whisk in the oil, parsley, salt, and pepper, and pour this mixture into the bowl. Add the mushrooms, and toss gently to coat thoroughly with oil mixture. Leave at room temperature until the mixture is cool, and then cover with plastic wrap, and refrigerate at least 5 hours or overnight.

To serve — arrange lettuce leaves on small plates and place some of the mushrooms topped with a little of the dressing on each plate.

Nutrient Values:

Calories:	48.3	Cholesterol:	0 mg
Protein:	1.86 g	Fiber:	1.61 g
Carbohydrates:	4.84 g	% Fat Calories:	28
Total Fat:	1.51 g		

Mushrooms

History: Mushrooms were first cultivated in France in the 1700's. Commercial cultivation was started in the U.S. in 1890.

Purchase: Select mushrooms with closed caps. If the cap is open and the dark fluting exposed, the mushrooms may have lost some of their moisture.

Store: Refrigerate in a plastic bag left open for the air to circulate; they will keep several days.

To Prepare: Never wash mushrooms! They absorb water like a sponge and will exude this liquid into your sauce or dish causing it to become watery. Just wipe them with a damp paper towel or a mushroom brush (purchased at any store that sells gourmet gadgets.)

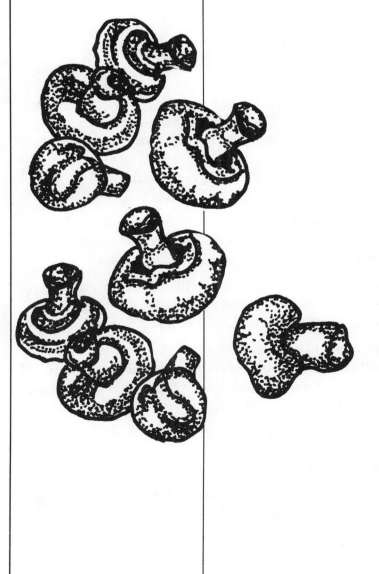

Stuffed Clams

These clams can be served as an hors d'oeuvres or an appetizer for special occasions. They can be prepared several hours ahead up to the asterisk.

Makes 16 clams

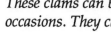

16 littleneck clams
1 teaspoon unsalted butter
1/4 cup finely chopped onion
2 tablespoons finely chopped sweet red pepper
2 cloves garlic, crushed
1/2 cup soft breadcrumbs, made from either whole wheat
   or oat bran bread
2 teaspoons lemon juice
1 1/2 teaspoons finely chopped fresh oregano, or 1/2 teaspoon dried
1 1/2 teaspoons finely chopped fresh basil, or 1/2 teaspoon dried
freshly ground black pepper
1 1/2 tablespoons freshly grated Parmesan cheese
1 tablespoon finely chopped fresh parsley

Method

Thoroughly wash the clams. Place in a vegetable steamer, and steam over simmering water for 8-10 minutes, or until the clams open. Reserve 1/4 cup of the clam juice. Discard the top shell, remove the meat from the bottom shell, and drain the bottom shell on paper towels. Mince the clams and set aside.

Lightly spray a small skillet with cooking spray, and melt the butter over medium heat. Saute the onion for 2 minutes, add red pepper, and garlic, and continue to saute until vegetables are tender. Set aside.

Strain the reserved clam juice, and combine with clams and sauteed vegetables in a medium sized bowl. Add the breadcrumbs, lemon juice, oregano, basil, and pepper. Stir well to mix.

Divide the mixture evenly among the clam shell halves, and arrange in a shallow baking dish. Mix together the Parmesan cheese, and parsley in a small bowl, and sprinkle over the tops of the stuffed clams.* If preparing ahead, cover and refrigerate.

Bake at 400 degrees for 8-10 minutes until thoroughly heated.

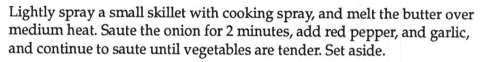

Nutrient Values:

Calories:	16.5	Cholesterol:	4.02 mg
Protein:	1.53 g	Fiber:	0.102 g
Carbohydrates:	1.36 g	% Fat Calories:	30
Total Fat:	0.539 g		

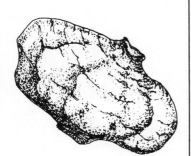

Jicama in Creamy Mustard Dressing

Jicama, is an ugly duckling, that when peeled becomes a beautiful swan! It is sweet and crunchy, and just delicious, either alone in a salad such as this one, or as part of a tossed salad. It is also wonderful as a component of a crudite arrangement.

Serves 4

2 teaspoons golden mustard seeds
1 tablespoon Dijon mustard
1 1/2 tablespoons red wine vinegar, mixed with 1 teaspoon honey
1/2 cup plain nonfat yogurt
1 pound coarsely grated jicama
salt and pepper to taste

Method

In a small non-stick saute pan, heat the mustard seeds for a few seconds, until they begin to pop. Transfer seeds to a small bowl, and then mix in the mustard, vinegar, and yogurt.

Place the jicama in a serving bowl, and then add the dressing, and toss well to mix. Serve immediately.

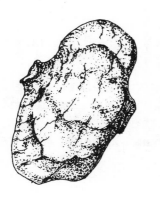

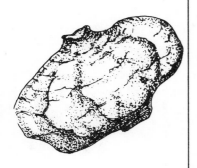

Nutrient Values:

Calories:	40	Cholesterol:	.500 mg
Protein:	2.15 g	Fiber:	1.25 g
Carbohydrates:	7.50 g	% Fat Calories:	2
Total Fat:	.094 g		

Crab Souffles

These delicious souffles are easy to make, and quite tasty.

Serves 6

6 ounces crabmeat
1 egg yolk
3/4 teaspoon fresh lemon juice
3/4 cup plain nonfat yogurt
2 teaspoons Hungarian paprika
1/4 teaspoon salt
pinch white pepper
6 egg whites

Method

Preheat the oven to 350 degrees. Lightly spray 6 ramekin dishes with cooking spray, and set aside.

In a large bowl, mix together the crabmeat, egg yolk, lemon juice, yogurt, paprika, salt and pepper.

In an electric mixer, using the whisk attachment, beat the egg whites until stiff buy not dry. Gently fold them into the crabmeat mixture. Divide the mixture between the prepared ramekin dishes, and place them in a baking pan. Bake the souffles for 16-18 minutes, or until they are golden.

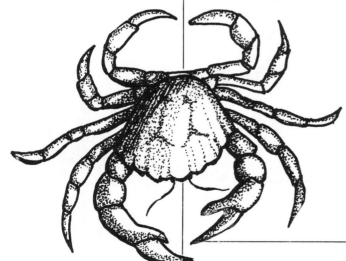

Nutrient Values:

Calories:	71.4	Cholesterol:	74.2 mg
Protein:	11.2 g	Fiber:	0 g
Carbohydrates:	2.59 g	% Fat Calories:	20
Total Fat:	1.49 g		

Tomato Salsa with Papayas and Pears

If you use ripe, juicy, fruits and vegetables, you will have a good flavored oil-free salsa. This is very good served as a dip, and is also excellent with grilled chicken or fish.

Makes 6 cups

2 very ripe pears, peeled, and finely chopped
1 ripe papaya, peeled, and finely chopped
6 very ripe tomatoes, seeded, and finely chopped
6 green onions, (scallions), finely chopped
8 ounces canned, chopped, green chilies
3 very large garlic cloves, chopped
juice of 2 limes
 1 teaspoon salt or to taste
freshly ground black pepper

Method

Combine all ingredients in a large bowl and stir well to mix. Let marinate in refrigerator for several hours or overnight. Taste, and adjust seasonings if necessary.

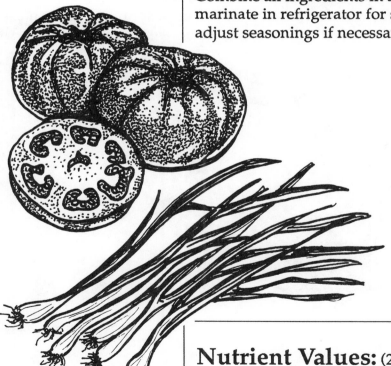

Nutrient Values: (2 tablespoons)

Calories:	13.2	Cholesterol:	0 mg
Protein:	0.319 g	Fiber:	0.755 g
Carbohydrates:	3.17 g	% Fat Calories:	7
Total Fat:	0.113 g		

Easy Salmon Mousse

I have been making this mousse for years, and everyone who likes salmon loves it! I serve it with crackers or crudites on a small silver tray that has been covered with lettuce.

Serves 8

1 envelope unflavored gelatin
2 tablespoons lemon juice
1 small onion, sliced
1/2 cup boiling water
1/2 teaspoon paprika
1 tablespoon fresh dill or 1 teaspoon dry dill
1-1 pound can sockeye salmon, drained, skin and bones removed
 1 1/2 cups nonfat yogurt
parsley (for garnish)

Method

Place first 4 ingredients in a blender or food processor and blend until onion is pureed. Add next 3 ingredients and blend again. Add the yogurt, 1/3 at a time and blend until very smooth. Lightly spray a 1 quart mold with non-stick spray, and pour the mixture into it. Chill for several hours or overnight. Decorate with parsley.

Nutrient Values:

Calories:	106	Cholesterol:	20.9 mg
Protein:	12.9 g	Fiber:	0.504 g
Carbohydrates:	5.21 g	% Fat Calories:	31
Total Fat:	3.54 g		

Bean Dip with Lemon Juice

This quick and easy bean dip is not spicy, and any leftover beans can be used to make this. It is also good as a stuffing for celery, or serve it with any other vegetables.

Serves 6

1 1/2 cups cooked kidney beans
2 teaspoons safflower oil
3 tablespoons finely chopped green onions
1 tablespoon finely chopped cilantro or parsley
1 tablespoon lemon juice
2 tablespoons chicken stock
3-4 dashes tabasco sauce
salt and pepper to taste

Method

Place beans in a blender or food processor, and process to a smooth paste. Add remaining ingredients, and refrigerate until very cold.

Nutrient Values:

Calories:	72.3	Cholesterol:	0.021 mg
Protein:	4.03 g	Fiber:	3.87 g
Carbohydrates:	10.6 g	% Fat Calories:	22
Total Fat:	1.73 g		

Creamy Clam Dip

This is a very good tasting dip, but be sure to allow it to sit in the refrigerator for at least 3 hours in order to allow the flavors to blend.

Serves 8

1 1/2 cups yogurt cheese (see page 40)
10 ounces minced clams, drained
1/4 cup chopped scallions (green onions)
1 1/4 teaspoons Dijon-style mustard
1/2 teaspoon Worcestershire sauce
1/4 teaspoon salt
Dash pepper

Method

In a medium size bowl combine all ingredients and stir well to mix. Refrigerate, covered for at least 3 hours. Taste and adjust seasonings as necessary.

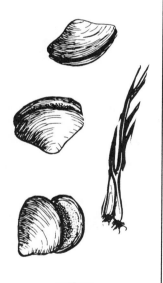

Nutrient Values:

Calories:	118	Cholesterol:	25.7 mg
Protein:	15.6 g	Fiber:	0.092 g
Carbohydrates:	10.9 g	% Fat Calories:	7
Total Fat:	.933 g		

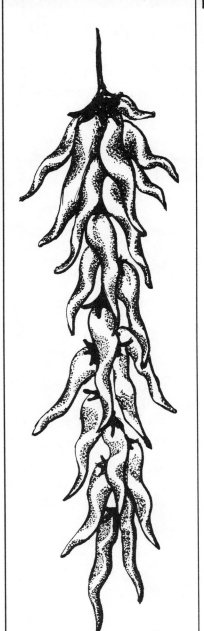

Hot and Spicy Dip

Whip up this low fat, high fiber, delicious dip, in just a couple of minutes.

Serves 10

2 cups red kidney beans
1 cup mild or medium hot chili salsa

Method

Puree in a blender or food processor. Serve with crudites.

Nutrient Values: (1/4 cup)

Calories:	63.6	Cholesterol:	0 mg
Protein:	3.47 g	Fiber:	3.70 g
Carbohydrates:	10.2 g	% Fat Calories:	18
Total Fat:	1.32 g		

Horseradish and Onion Yogurt Dip

I like to use fresh horseradish when I make this dip. If you are not used to using it, start off with only 2 tablespoons and add more according to your taste.

Serves 6

1 cup nonfat yogurt
2 tablespoons lite mayonaise
3 tablespoons tomato paste
4 tablespoons fresh or prepared horseradish
1 tablespoon onion flakes
1 teaspoon garlic powder
1/2 teaspoon sugar
salt and pepper to taste

Method

In a medium bowl combine all ingredients and stir well to mix. Refrigerate, covered for at least 1 hour to blend flavors.

Nutrient Values:

Calories:	48.4	Cholesterol:	1.88 mg
Protein:	2.75 g	Fiber:	0.501 g
Carbohydrates:	7.35 g	% Fat Calories:	20
Total Fat:	1.13 g		

Salmon Spread

This delicious spread can be prepared in advance, covered, and stored in the refrigerator. I like to serve it in the center of an attractive tray, surrounded by assorted crudites.

Serves 14

1 pound skinned, drained, canned salmon, flaked
1 cup yogurt cheese (see page 40)
4 whole scallions, trimmed, and finely minced
1 tablespoon lemon juice
1 tablespoon Dijon mustard
1 tablespoon prepared horseradish
salt and pepper to taste

Method

In a medium sized bowl, combine all ingredients, and stir well to mix. Cover and refrigerate for at least 1 hour before using.

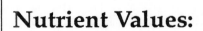

Nutrient Values:

Calories:	73.4	Cholesterol:	12.5 mg
Protein:	8.71g	Fiber:	0.014 g
Carbohydrates:	4.52g	% Fat Calories:	26
Total Fat:	2.08 g		

Honey Popcorn Balls

Try this delicious low calorie, high fiber treat next time you are in a "snacking mood".

Serves 4

4 cups airpopped popcorn
3 tablespoons honey
1 teaspoon vanilla

Method

Combine honey and vanilla in a medium sized saucepan and heat the honey to liquidity. Add the popcorn and toss well to coat evenly.

VARIATION: Add 1 teaspoon cinnamon to the honey and vanilla mixture.

Nutrient Values:

Calories:	78.3	Cholesterol:	0 mg
Protein:	1.05 g	Fiber:	1.30 g
Carbohydrates:	19.1 g	% Fat Calories:	4
Total Fat:	0.400 g		

Super Spicy Popcorn

Vary the seasonings in this recipe to make a variety of different popcorn treats.

Serves 4

4 cups airpopped popcorn
1 teaspoon chili powder
1 teaspoon curry powder
1/2 teaspoon onion powder
1/2 teaspoon garlic powder

Method

Combine the seasonings in a small measuring cup or bowl. Add to the freshly popped popcorn, and toss well to mix.

Nutrient Values:

Calories:	35.3	Cholesterol:	0 mg
Protein:	1.23 g	Fiber:	1.71 g
Carbohydrates:	7.12 g	% Fat Calories:	14
Total Fat:	0.583 g		

Soups, Stews and Stocks

Soups and stews are ideal for lunch or dinner, and often need nothing more to accompany them than a crusty whole wheat roll, and a large tossed salad. They can save a lot of cooking time, since once prepared, they can happily be eaten for several days. They are an excellent source of vitamins, minerals and fiber, and the soups containing milk or yogurt are a good source of calcium.

Stocks, Soups and Stews

Soups and Stocks

A soup is only as good as the stock on which it is built, and homemade soup is really simple to make. The ingredients are simmered, strained, and then degreased, and the cooking liquid can be stored for use later on, or used on its own with the addition of rice or pasta.

When making soup it is important to remove the scum that forms on the surface, as this will cloud the stock. Do not allow the stock to return to the boil after the initial boiling, as boiling, instead of simmering the liquid will produce a cloudy stock.

Be sure to remove all of the fat before you freeze the stock, as frozen fat can turn rancid.

Soups are ideal for lunch, or dinner, and often need nothing more to accompany them, than a crusty whole wheat roll, and a large tossed salad. Soups provide a good source of vitamins, minerals, and fiber.

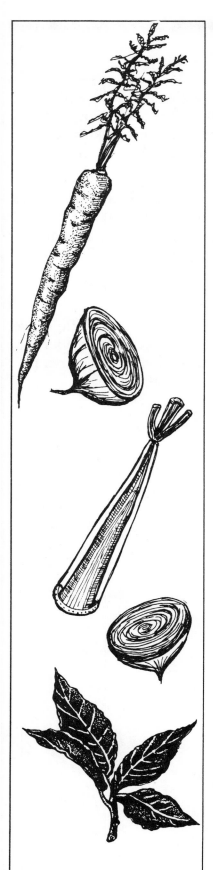

Chicken Stock

This is a good basic stock to use for all of the soup recipes in this book. I like to freeze some of the stock in ice cube trays, and once frozen, place the cubes in plastic freezer bags, to use when I only need a small amount of stock.

Makes 3 quarts

3 pounds uncooked, skinless chicken thighs
2 pounds uncooked, skinless chicken drumsticks
3 raw carrots, sliced into 1/2 inch rounds
3 celery stalks, sliced into 1 inch pieces
2 large onions, cut into quarters, 1 quarter stuck with 2 whole cloves
2 sprigs fresh thyme, or 1/2 teaspoon dried thyme
2 bay leaves
10 sprigs fresh parsley
6 peppercorns
3-4 chicken necks, gizzards, and hearts (optional, the necks are rich in gelatin, and will produce a more gelatinous stock)

Method

Put all of the meat, (including necks, gizzards, and heart if desired), in a large stock pot, with enough water to cover them by about 2 inches. Bring the liquid to a slow boil, and skim off the scum that forms on the surface. Simmer for 10 minutes, skimming as necessary. Add the vegetables, herbs, and peppercorns, covering them with additional water if needed. Reduce the heat to low, and simmer for 3 hours, skimming once more.

Strain the stock, and when cool, refrigerate it overnight. Remove any fat that has congealed.

The stock will keep for 3-4 days, covered, and refrigerated, or may be frozen for up to 6 months in freezer containers.

Nutrient Values:

Nutritional analysis is not available, since all meat, vegetables, and fat are removed at the end of the cooking time.

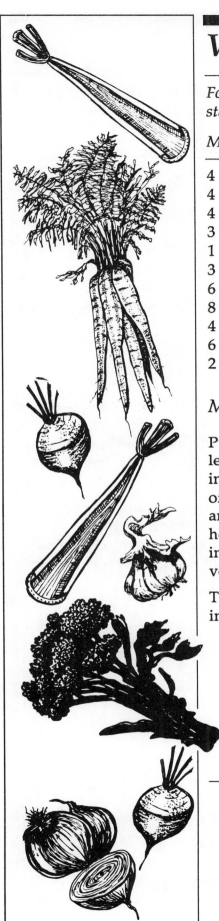

Vegetable Stock

For vegetarians, this stock is invaluable when making soups, and/or stews.

Makes about 2 quarts

4 celery stalks with leaves, cut into 1-inch pieces
4 carrots, washed, unpeeled, and cut into 1-inch pieces
4 large onions, cut into quarters
3 large broccoli stems, coarsely chopped
1 small turnip, peeled, and cut into large dice
3 cabbage leaves, coarsely shredded
6 large garlic cloves, crushed
8 black peppercorns
4 fresh thyme sprigs, or 1 teaspoon dried thyme
6 fresh parsley sprigs
2 bay leaves, crumbled

Method

Put all of the ingredients except the thyme, parsley, and bay leaves into a stockpot. Pour in enough cold water to cover the ingredients by about 2 inches. Bring the liquid to a boil, and skim off any scum that forms on the surface. Add the thyme, parsley, and bay leaves, reduce the heat, and let the stock simmer for 1 hour. Strain the stock, pressing down the vegetables as you do so in order to extract as much of their juices as possible. Discard the vegetables.

The stock may be refrigerated, covered, for several days, or frozen in freezer containers.

Nutrient Values:

Nutritional analysis is not available, since all meat, vegetables, and fat are removed at the end of the cooking time.

Apple Soup

This delightful soup is low in cholesterol and is a good source of fiber. It would be good to serve at a luncheon or before a heavy main meal.

Serves 4

4 apples
1 cup apple juice
juice of 1 lemon
1 cinnamon stick
1/2 tablespoon honey
1/4 teaspoon vanilla
1 cup orange juice
1 cup nonfat yogurt to which 2 teaspoons honey has been added
2 tablespoons Triple Sec

Method

Peel, core, and quarter 3 of the apples. Combine with apple juice, lemon juice, honey, cinnamon stick and vanilla in a large saucepan. Cover, and cook for about 20 minutes over medium heat. Let the apples cool, then cover and refrigerate for at least two hours or overnight.

Remove cinnamon stick. Add the orange juice and the nonfat yogurt to the apples, and puree in batches in a blender or food processor. Shred remaining unpeeled apple into the chilled mixture along with the liqueur. Stir gently, just to incorporate, and serve at cool room temperature.

Nutrient Values:

Calories:	183	Cholesterol:	1.00 mg
Protein:	3.98 g	Fiber:	3.06 g
Carbohydrates:	41.1 g	% Fat Calories:	4
Total Fat:	0.730 g		

Strawberry Soup

This delicious soup would be wonderful to serve at a ladies' luncheon. It has been my experience that most men dislike cold soups (especially fruit soups) quite vehemently.

Serves 4

---

1 1/2 cups water
3/4 cup light-bodied wine
1/3 cup sugar
2 tablespoons fresh lemon juice
1 stick cinnamon
1 quart strawberries, stemmed and pureed
1 cup nonfat yogurt to which 2 teaspoons honey has been added

Method

Combine water, wine, lemon juice, and cinnamon in a 3 quart saucepan, and simmer, uncovered for about 15 minutes, stirring occasionally. Add the strawberry puree and simmer, stirring frequently, 10 minutes more. Discard cinnamon stick and cool.

Add the nonfat yogurt mixture, and fold into the strawberry mixture. Serve at cool room temperature.

Nutrient Values:

Calories:	207	Cholesterol:	1.00 mg
Protein:	4.72 g	Fiber:	5.92 g
Carbohydrates:	40.7 g	% Fat Calories:	4
Total Fat:	0.961 g		

Blueberry Soup

This delicately flavored soup is a wonderful way to start off a luncheon. Arrowroot is used instead of cornstarch in order that the soup will not become cloudy when thickened.

Serves 4

1 1/2 cups fresh or frozen blueberries
1 1/2 cups water
1 cup unsweetened grape juice
1 tablespoon honey
3 teaspoons arrowroot

Method

Combine blueberries, 1 cup water, grape juice, and honey in a medium saucepan. Cover and simmer over low heat for about 5 minutes. DO NOT OVERCOOK. Dissolve arrowroot in remaining 1/2 cup water and stir into the soup. Cook stirring constantly until the mixture comes to a boil. Remove from the heat and cool. Refrigerate, covered, until chilled.

Nutrient Values:

Calories:	91.3	Cholesterol:	0 mg
Protein:	0.618 g	Fiber:	1.68 g
Carbohydrates:	22.7 g	% Fat Calories:	4
Total Fat:	0.431 g		

Cold Peach and Wine Soup

This is a good soup to make in the summertime when the peaches are ripe and juicy.

Serves 6

1 cup water
3 tablespoons sugar
1 teaspoon whole cloves
1 cinnamon stick
1 tablespoon plus 2 teaspoons arrowroot dissolved in 2 cups dry white wine
2 pounds fresh peaches, pureed

Method

Combine first 4 ingredients in a medium saucepan and bring to boil over medium heat. Reduce the heat, cover the pan, and simmer the mixture for 30 minutes. Strain and return to the pan. Dissolve the arrowroot in the wine, being careful to dissolve any lumps, and blend into the contents of the pan. Bring to a boil, stirring occasionally. Let cool, then add the pureed peaches. Chill well before serving.

Variation 1: Substitute sweet, ripe pears for the peaches.

Variation 2: Substitute nectarines for the peaches

Nutrient Values:

Calories:	149	Cholesterol:	0 mg
Protein:	1.15 g	Fiber:	2.63 g
Carbohydrates:	25.4 g	% Fat Calories:	1
Total Fat:	0.152 g		

Southwestern Vegetable Soup

This fast and easy soup can be made in minutes with a food processor. Add carrots and celery if you like, but be sure to use a good, strong chicken stock (homemade is best) or the soup will be sadly lacking in flavor.

Serves 6

3 large ripe tomatoes, peeled, seeded and cut in half
1/2 medium red onion, sliced
1 medium white Spanish onion, sliced
1 green pepper, seeded
1 red pepper, seeded
2 cloves garlic, mashed
4 cups chicken stock
1 1/2 teaspoons Hungarian paprika
2 tablespoons tomato paste
1/2 teaspoon salt
1/2 cup fresh orange juice
1 tablespoon fresh lemon juice
4 tablespoons long grain rice

Method

Coarsely chop the first six ingredients. Add all the remaining ingredients except for the rice, and put in a large pot. Bring to a boil, reduce the heat, and simmer for 15 minutes. Add the rice and simmer 15 minutes longer.

Variation: Add skinless chicken thighs when you add the rice, and cook until chicken thighs are tender.

Nutrient Values:

Calories:	105	Cholesterol:	0.667 mg
Protein:	5.63 g	Fiber:	2.87 g
Carbohydrates:	18.2 g	% Fat Calories:	13
Total Fat:	1.59 g		

Cream of Carrot and Apple Soup

This unusual soup in very spicy and flavorful.

Serves 6

1 1/2 pound carrots cut into thin rounds
2 teaspoons safflower oil
2 onions chopped (about 1 1/2 cups)
2 large apples, unpeeled, cored, and thinly sliced
1/4 cup grated fresh ginger
6 cups good flavored chicken stock
1/2 teaspoon salt
freshly ground black pepper
1/2 cup nonfat yogurt
2 tablespoons freshly chopped parsley

Method

Heat oil in a large, non-stick pot over medium heat. Add onions and cook them, stirring occasionally until they are golden, about 10 minutes. Add the carrots, ginger and apples and stir in chicken stock, salt and pepper. Reduce the heat, cover the pot, and cook until the carrots are tender, about twenty minutes.

Let the soup cool a little before pureeing in batches in a blender or food processor. Add the yogurt, and reheat a little if necessary, being sure not to allow the mixture to boil. Add the freshly chopped parsley, and serve immediately.

Time Saver: Omit the apples and add one cup of applesauce to the pureed mixture before heating through.

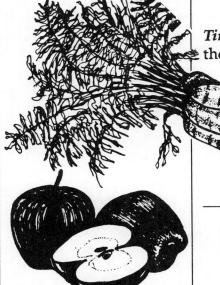

Nutrient Values:

Calories:	172	Cholesterol:	1.33 mg
Protein:	7.94 g	Fiber:	6.45 g
Carbohydrates:	28.4 g	% Fat Calories:	18
Total Fat:	3.54 g		

Hot and Sour Soup

This unusual tasting soup has a wonderful Oriental flavor. Serve it as an appetizer in small bowls.

Serves 4

4 cups chicken stock
2 tablespoons rice vinegar
1 tablespoon red wine vinegar
5 drops hot red-pepper sauce
1 tablespoon low-sodium soy sauce
1 tablespoon dry sherry
1 teaspoon finely chopped garlic
1 tablespoon finely chopped fresh ginger
1 carrot, cut into fine dice
4 shiitake or chinese black mushroom caps, covered with boiling water and soaked for 20 minutes, then thinly sliced
1 tablespoon arrowroot mixed with 2 tablespoons cold water
4 ounces firm bean curd (tofu) cut into thin strips
2 scallions, trimmed and sliced

Method

Heat the stock in a large pot over medium heat. Add the vinegars, hot red-pepper sauce, soy sauce, sherry, garlic, ginger, carrot and shiitake mushrooms. Bring the mixture to a boil, and then stir in the arrowroot mixture. Reduce the heat, and simmer the soup for one minute, stirring constantly. Gently stir in the bean curd. Serve, garnishing with the scallion slices.

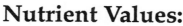

Nutrient Values:

Calories:	77.6	Cholesterol:	0.750 mg
Protein:	6.74 g	Fiber:	1.72 g
Carbohydrates:	6.90 g	% Fat Calories:	29
Total Fat:	2.49 g		

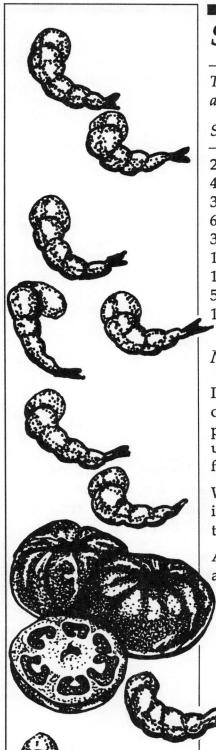

Spicy Tomato and Shrimp Soup

This soup is quite spicy! Be careful to cook the shrimp only until they are just done — or they will be tough and rubbery.

Serves 4

2 teaspoons safflower oil
4 tablespoons minced onions
3 cups unsalted chicken stock
6 large, ripe tomatoes, or 1-1 pound can tomatoes, including their juice
3 tablespoons red wine vinegar
1/4 teaspoon white pepper
1 teaspoon Dijon mustard
5 drops hot red-pepper sauce
1 pound medium or small shrimp, shelled and deveined

Method

In a non-stick 2-3 quart pan, heat 1 teaspoon of the oil. Saute onion until limp, and then add chicken stock, tomatoes, vinegar, pepper, mustard, and hot red-pepper sauce. Simmer for 10 minutes. Remove from heat, allow to cool slightly, and puree in a food processor. Return to the pan, and reheat if necessary.

While the soup in simmering, saute the shrimp in a non-stick pan in the other teaspoon oil. Be careful to cook only until the shrimp turns pink.

Add the cooked shrimp to the pureed soup, and serve immediately.

Nutrient Values:

Calories:	133	Cholesterol:	111 mg
Protein:	16.7 g	Fiber:	1.83 g
Carbohydrates:	7.10 g	% Fat Calories:	29
Total Fat:	4.25 g		

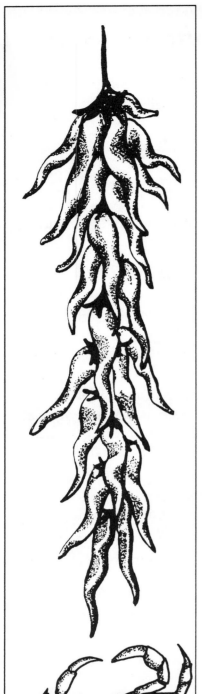

Seafood Gazpacho

This excellent soup can be served for lunch, or as a main meal on a hot summer day.

Serves 10

1 cup fresh breadcrumbs
3 cloves garlic minced
1 cucumber, peeled, seeded, and cut into 1/4 inch dices
2 sweet red peppers, cored, seeded, and chopped
1 medium sized red onion, chopped
5 ripe tomatoes, seeded and chopped
3 jalepeño peppers, cored, seeded and chopped
5 cups tomato juice
1/2 cup fresh lime juice (4 limes)
1/4 cup olive oil
1 tablespoon ground cumin
salt and freshly ground black pepper to taste
1 pound flaked crabmeat

Method

Combine the breadcrumbs and garlic and set aside. Combine the cucumber, red peppers, jalepeño peppers, onion, and tomatoes in a large bowl. Pour in the tomato juice and the lime juice and stir to combine. Add the breadcrumb mixture, and stir in the oil.

Puree half of the soup in a food processor or a blender, and then stir back into the half that has not been pureed. Season with cumin and salt and pepper to taste. Refrigerate until cold.

Just before serving stir in the crabmeat.

Nutrient Values:

Calories:	159	Cholesterol:	45.4 mg
Protein:	12.3 g	Fiber:	3.60 g
Carbohydrates:	17.3 g	% Fat Calories:	30
Total Fat:	5.63 g		

Cream of Broccoli Soup

This soup is made very quickly and is quite delicious. Just be sure to use a good flavored chicken stock.

Serves 6

1 quart chicken stock
2 small onions, coarsely chopped
3 cloves garlic, peeled
1 1/4 pounds, (about 5 cups) broccoli, coarsely chopped
1 1/2 cups low fat milk
salt and freshly ground pepper
pinch nutmeg

Method

In a large saucepan, combine stock, onions and garlic. Bring to a boil and simmer for 15 minutes. Add the broccoli, and simmer until tender, about 5 minutes.

Cool slightly, and then puree the soup in a blender or food processor. Return to saucepan. Add the milk, salt, pepper, and nutmeg. Serve hot or cold.

Nutrient Values:

Calories:	96.5	Cholesterol:	6.17 mg
Protein:	8.01 g	Fiber:	3.17 g
Carbohydrates:	11.9 g	% Fat Calories:	22
Total Fat:	2.48 g		

Vegetable Soup

The vegetables in this soup can be varied according to the season and/or whatever you may have on hand.

Serves 8

6 cups good flavored, chicken stock
2 cups chopped leeks (white portion) or onion
3/4 teaspoon minced garlic
1 cup celery, finely sliced
1 cup tomatoes, peeled, seeded, and chopped
1 cup broccoli flowerets
1 cup zucchini, diced
1/4 cup small pasta such as tubettini
1-2 tablespoons chopped fresh herbs (such as parsley, oregano, or basil)
salt and freshly ground pepper

Method

Measure the chicken stock into a large saucepan. Add the leeks or onions, garlic, celery, and tomatoes, and simmer for about 8-10 minutes. Add broccoli, cauliflower, zucchini, and pasta, and cook until tender, about 8-10 minutes. Stir in herbs and season to taste with salt and pepper. Serve immediately.

Nutrient Values:

Calories:	66.0	Cholesterol:	0.750 mg
Protein:	5.35 g	Fiber:	2.16 g
Carbohydrates:	8.75 g	% Fat Calories:	17
Total Fat:	1.29 g		

Chicken and Capellini Soup

This excellent soup can be served as a complete lunch, or as an appetizer. Be careful to only allow the soup to simmer, boiling it will make the chicken tough, and break up the tofu.

Serves 6

12 ounces boneless breast of chicken, skin removed, and cut into cubes
2 tablespoons low-sodium soy sauce
2 tablespoons red port
3 ounces capellini, broken into 1 inch lengths
12 cups chicken stock
3 carrots, thinly sliced
2 red peppers, thinly sliced
4 stalks celery, thinly sliced
6 garlic cloves, finely chopped
3 scallions, thinly sliced
12 ounces firm tofu (bean curd) cut into thin strips

Method

Combine chicken, soy sauce and port in a bowl. Cover and marinate for at least one hour.

Meanwhile, bring about five cups of water to a rolling boil, and add 1/2 teaspoon of salt and the capellini. Test the pasta after two minutes and only cook until al dente. Drain pasta, rinse under cold water to prevent it from sticking together and set aside.

Bring stock to boil in a large pot. Add the carrots, peppers, celery, and garlic cloves, and simmer for about 5 minutes, or until almost tender. Add the chicken and its marinade, tofu, and capellini. Continue to simmer the soup until the chicken is cooked, only about two or three minutes. Season to taste, and serve immediately.

Nutrient Values:

Calories:	244	Cholesterol:	34.7 mg
Protein:	29.5 g	Fiber:	2.97 g
Carbohydrates:	15.0 g	% Fat Calories:	25
Total Fat:	6.59 g		

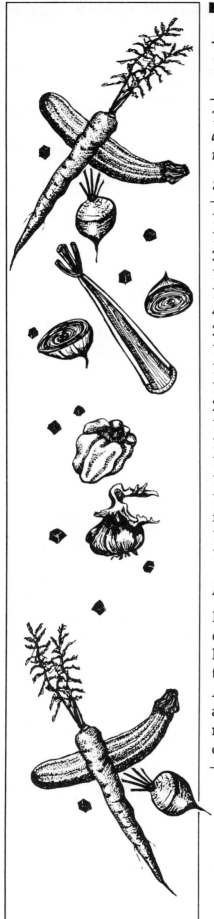

Hearty Burgundy Beef and Vegetable Stew

This soup has a very good flavor, and the vegetables can be varied according to whatever you may have on hand at the time. It can also be made without the meat.

Serves 8

1 teaspoon safflower oil
1 medium onion, sliced very thin
2 garlic cloves, finely minced
1/2 cup red wine, preferably a hearty burgundy
1 tablespoon chopped fresh thyme, (or 1 teaspoon dried thyme)
4 cups beef stock
2 carrots, cut into 3/4 inch pieces
1 1/2 cups cauliflower flowerettes
1 small yellow squash, halved lengthwise and cut into 3/4 inch cubes
1 zucchini, halved lengthwise and cut into 3/4 inch pieces
2 stalks celery, sliced into 3/4 inch pieces
1 small turnip, cut into 3/4 inch cubes
1 sweet red pepper, seeded, deribbed and cut into 3/4 inch squares
1-1pound can tomatoes, including their juice
1 cup coarsely shredded red cabbage
1/2 teaspoon salt
freshly ground black pepper
10 ounces boneless sirloin, cut into small cubes
1/4 cup long grain rice

Method

Heat the oil in a large, non-stick pot over medium heat. Cook the onions in the hot oil until they are soft, about 5 minutes. Add the garlic and continue to cook for 1 minute more. Pour in the red wine, add the thyme and bring the mixture to a boil, then cook for 1 minute. Add the beef stock and bring to a boil. Add all the vegetables, salt and pepper, and gently simmer for 15 minutes. Add the meat and rice and continue to barely simmer 15-20 minutes more or until rice is cooked. Serve in large bowls with dark bread.

Nutrient Values:

Calories:	179	Cholesterol:	27.4 mg
Protein:	14.8 g	Fiber:	4.61 g
Carbohydrates:	18.9 g	% Fat Calories:	23
Total Fat:	4.55 g		

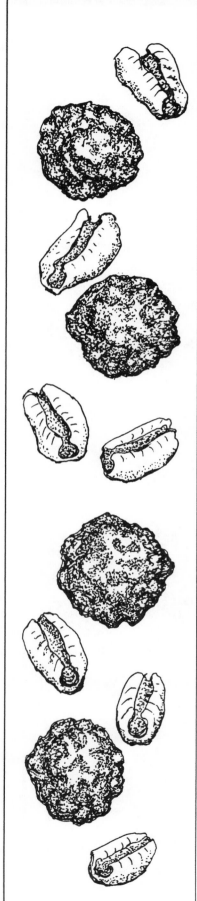

Meatball Stew with Macaroni and Fresh Herbs

Making this stew with ground turkey meat reduces the fat considerably. However, since ground turkey meat has very little flavor of it's own, it is important to mix together all of the meatball ingredients, and allow the mixture to sit in the refrigerator for at least 30 minutes. This together with cooking the meatballs in a good flavored beef stock will ensure you a tasty, low fat stew.

Serves 6

12 ounces ground turkey meat
2 beaten egg whites
1 1/2 tablespoons chopped fresh basil
1 1/2 tablespoons chopped fresh oregano
2 slices day old bread, crumbled
2 tomatoes, finely chopped
1/2 cup onion, finely chopped
6 garlic gloves, finely chopped
1/2 teaspoon salt
freshly ground black pepper
8 cups good flavored beef stock
2 carrots, thinly sliced
2 stalks celery, thinly sliced
1 cup tomato juice
4 ounces small shell macaroni, uncooked

Method

In a large bowl, combine the turkey, egg whites, oregano, basil, bread, tomato, onion, garlic, salt, and freshly ground black pepper. Cover the bowl with plastic wrap and refrigerate for 30 minutes or longer. Form the chilled mixture into meatballs, about 1" in diameter and set aside. Pour the stock into a large pot. Add the carrots, celery and tomato juice, and simmer the liquid over medium heat for about 10 minutes.

Add the meatballs carefully to the simmering stock. Cook for about 5 minutes before adding the macaroni, and continue to allow the mixture to simmer gently for another 10 minutes. Taste, and adjust seasonings. Transfer the soup to individual bowls and serve immediately.

Nutrient Values:

Calories:	170	Cholesterol:	30.4 mg
Protein:	15.3 g	Fiber:	2.34 g
Carbohydrates:	15.0 g	% Fat Calories:	29
Total Fat:	5.61 g		

Your Notes:

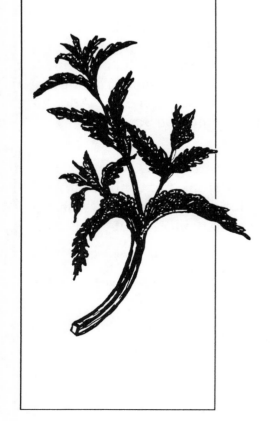

Omelettes

An omelette is a good lunch or dinner dish, and is an excellent way to use up all kinds of leftovers. Since eggs are high in cholesterol, limit the number that you eat.

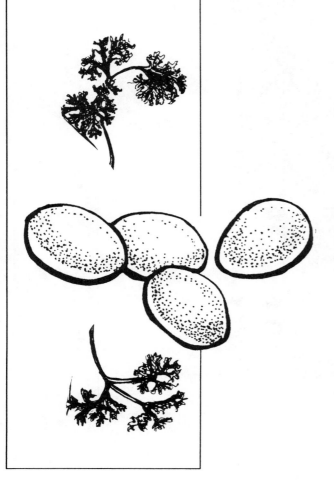

Omelettes

How To Make An Omelet

(It takes longer to describe how to make an omelet than it does to actually cook it!)

Making a good omelet takes practice, so don't be discouraged if your omelet is not perfect on the first try.

The pan that you use to make the omelet should be the size indicated in the recipe, and for our purposes non-stick. For a 2 or 3 egg omelet, sufficient for 1 portion, a 5-6 inch skillet is recommended. If the pan is too small you will have a thick and under-cooked omelet, and a too large pan gives a thin omelet that is easily over-cooked.

Cold eggs are harder to overcook; room-temperature eggs make a fluffier omelet, but whichever you use be sure you don't over-beat the eggs. In a small bowl, using a fork, mix together egg whites, whole eggs, and water; mix only until ingredients are mingled lightly. If you overbeat at this stage you will have a tough omelet.

Lightly spray the pan with non-stick cooking spray, and turn the heat to medium-high. Let the pan heat up, then pour in the egg mixture all at once. Stir the eggs with a heat-proof plastic fork or wooden spatula, as if you were making scrambled eggs. As the omelet begins to cook, lift it up at the edges to allow the uncooked egg to run underneath. When the eggs are almost cooked, turn off the heat, and place the filling across the center of the omelet in a line with the handle of the pan. Loosen one side of the omelet with a spatula, and fold it about a third over the remainder. Hold the pan over the warm serving plate so the other side begins to slip out. Flip omelet so that the previously folded side folds over. You should now have an omelet folded into thirds with the center third on top.

VARIATIONS:

Mushroom and Yogurt Omelet: Mix together 3 tablespoons yogurt cheese, 4 tablespoons sauteed mushrooms, salt and pepper to taste, and 1 tablespoon finely minced fresh herbs such as tarragon or dill.

Ratatouille Omelet: Spoon hot ratatouille in the omelet, and top with freshly chopped parsley.

Tomato, Onion, and Potato Omelet: Saute a small onion in a non-stick pan, and add 1 diced tomato, and 1 diced, cooked potato. sprinkle with 1 tablespoon fresh herbs.

Strawberry Blintz Omelets

This delicate omelet is filled with yogurt cheese (see page 40), and brown sugar, and covered with strawberries. Serve it for breakfast with juice, or try it sometime for lunch accompanied with fresh fruit.

Serves 1

1/2 cup strawberries

Filling
4 teaspoons light brown sugar
3 tablespoons yogurt cream cheese
1 teaspoon 2% lowfat milk
pinch nutmeg

Omelet
2 egg whites
1 large egg
2 teaspoon cold water
6-inch non-stick skillet
warm serving plate

Method

Hull strawberries, reserving a few with leaves for garnish; cut the hulled berries in halves. Place in a bowl, mix lightly with 1 teaspoon of the light brown sugar.

In a separate bowl mix together the yogurt cheese, 2 teaspoons sugar, milk, and nutmeg. Beat until fluffy. Set aside.

Prepare the omelet as described on page 129, sprinkling the cheese mixture with the remaining teaspoon of brown sugar.

Serve on the warmed plate, and cover with the strawberries. Garnish with whole berries. Serve at once.

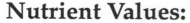

Nutrient Values:

Calories:	265	Cholesterol:	276 mg
Protein:	19.7 g	Fiber:	1.93 g
Carbohydrates:	33.0 g	% Fat Calories:	21
Total Fat:	6.06 g		

Vegetables, Legumes and Rice

You don't have to be a vegetarian to enjoy these high fiber, low fat dishes, but many of these recipes can be used as meatless entrees. Both from a health and cost point of view, eating more meatless lunches, and dinners can be very beneficial. Important information on buying and storing vegetables are included in this section, as well as the history of many of them.

Your Notes:

Vegetables, Legumes and Rice

About Beans

History: Beans have been used for over 9,000 years. The ancient Egyptians connected beans with death, and in medieval Europe dried peas and beans were associated with famine, since they were usually only eaten when there was little else to eat.

Nutrition: Beans provide more energy and protein than either root or green vegetables. They are a good source of fiber, B vitamin, calcium, phosphorus, potassium, and iron. They are valuable in any diet, and invaluable to vegetarians.

Yield: 1 pound packaged beans = 2 cups dry or 5-6 cups cooked. 1-15 1/2 ounce can (drained) = 1 2/3 cups cooked beans.

Washing: All beans should be thoroughly washed and inspected for damaged beans and foreign material before soaking.

Soaking Tips: Soaking shortens cooking time and improves flavor, texture, appearance and digestibility. The soak water should always be discarded, and the beans rinsed and cooked in fresh water.

Traditional Method: To 1 pound dry beans add 6 cups cold water and salt. Stand overnight or 6-8 hours. Do not refrigerate. Drain, rinse and cook.

Quick Method: To 1 pound dry beans, add 6-8 cups hot water, and salt if desired. Heat, let boil for 3 minutes, cover and set aside for 1 hour. Drain, rinse and cook.

Cooking:
Standard Method: Drain and rinse soaked beans; put into a large pot. Add 6 cups hot water, 1 tablespoon safflower oil, and salt if desired. Boil gently with lid tilted until tender.

Variation: A chopped onion, or onion powder, or garlic powder can be added with the hot water. Also stock or a mixture of stock and water can be used.

Cooking Hints: Adding oil prevents foaming.
Acid slows down cooking. Add tomatoes, vinegar, etc. towards the end of cooking time.

Spicy Beans

This delicious bean dish can also be used to make a burrito filling by cooking the ingredients uncovered, until thickened. Serve this with fajitas, or any other favorite Mexican dish.

Serves 4

1 cup dry, red kidney beans soaked several hours, or overnight
1 small ham bone, trimmed of all fat, or 3 ounces lean ham, cut into pieces
1 large onion, chopped
4 small red dry peppers, finely chopped
1/4 teaspoon salt
1 teaspoon fresh garlic, minced
1/4 teaspoon cumin

Method

Drain and rinse the beans. Add 2 cups fresh water, and all of the remaining ingredients. Cook in a crock pot for 10 hours, or in a 225 degree oven for 7-8 hours.

Nutrient Values:

Calories:	216	Cholesterol:	11.7 mg
Protein:	17.4 g	Fiber:	11.2 g
Carbohydrates:	34.1 g	% Fat Calories:	7
Total Fat:	1.73 g		

Beef and Bean Casserole

This delicious casserole is a good source of vitamins, minerals, and fiber. Serve this with one or two vegetables and a large tossed salad.

Serves 6-8

2 cups drained, cooked or canned red beans
2 cups drained, cooked or canned garbanzo beans
2 cups drained, cooked or canned lima beans
1/2 pound ground turkey meat
1/2 pound ground lean beef
1 large onion, chopped
1 clove garlic, minced
4 tablespoons brown sugar
2 tablespoons Dijon mustard
1/2 cup catsup
1 teaspoon cumin powder
1/4 cup Hearty Burgundy red wine, red Port, or 1/4 cup water
    mixed together with 3 tablespoons vinegar
salt and freshly ground pepper

Method

Put drained beans in a 2 1/2 quart casserole; set aside. In a large non-stick skillet, cook ground beef, onions and garlic until meat is lightly browned; stir in the remaining ingredients. Add skillet mixture to beans in the casserole and mix together. Cover and bake for 1 hour.

Nutrient Values:

Calories:	376	Cholesterol:	48.5 mg
Protein:	25.6 g	Fiber:	11.2 g
Carbohydrates:	44.4 g	% Fat Calories:	26
Total Fat:	10.8 g		

Old Fashioned Baked Beans

This recipe will allow you to enjoy the flavor of pork and beans without the customary fat. Consider making a big batch of this recipe and freezing the extra for future use.

Serves 8

2 cups dried white beans or navy beans
1 teaspoon salt
1 teaspoon dry mustard
1/2 teaspoon freshly ground black pepper
3 drops Tabasco
1 large onion, chopped
2 tablespoons dark molasses
2 tablespoons honey
2 tablespoons brown sugar
1/4 cup cider vinegar
1/4 pound Canadian bacon, cubed

Method

Cook the beans according to one of the three methods given in Western Style Baked Bean recipe. Drain, and combine warm beans with salt, mustard, black pepper and Tabasco. Stir in onion, molasses, honey, brown sugar and vinegar. Mix well to thoroughly coat beans.

Pour half of the mixture into a 2 quart casserole. Add half of the Canadian bacon and then the rest of the beans. Top with remaining bacon. Pour boiling water in to the top of the beans. Cover. Bake at 300 degrees for 6 hours if not planning to freeze, or, 5 hours if freezing.

Nutrient Values:

Calories:	238	Cholesterol:	8.14 mg
Protein:	13.4 g	Fiber:	14.6 g
Carbohydrates:	43.1 g	% Fat Calories:	7
Total Fat:	1.93 g		

Western Style Beans

This is a great way to have the flavor of ham without eating too much of it. The long, slow cooking develops the wonderful robust flavor of these beans, which should be cooked in either a slow-cooker or a large heavy pot with a lid.

Serves 8

1 pound small white, pink, red, or navy beans
1 ham hock or shank*
2 large onions, chopped
6 cups water
1/2 - 3/4 teaspoon salt
4 cups ripe tomatoes, peeled seeded and chopped, or 4 cups canned tomatoes

Method

Electric slow cooker: Rinse and sort beans. Put all ingredients in cooker and leave for at least 10 hours.

Stove top cooking: Heat all ingredients to boiling with pot uncovered. Turn down heat, cover and simmer gently, adding enough boiling water to keep beans covered. Simmer for 3 hours.

When beans are done, remove ham bone, cut off meat and put it back into the pot. Serve hot with cornbread or muffins.

*** Ham and Bacon**
Because of the nitrites in most ham, it should be eaten only occasionally, and in small amounts. This holds true for bacon also.

Nutrient Values:

Calories:	254	Cholesterol:	9.62 mg
Protein:	17.2 g	Fiber:	19.0 g
Carbohydrates:	43.2 g	% Fat Calories:	7
Total Fat:	2.06 g		

Southwestern Salad

Try this high fiber salad next time you make fajitas. Make it at least 1 hour before you plan to serve it, in order to allow the flavors to marinate.

Serves 6

Dressing

2 tablespoons olive oil
2 tablespoons red wine vinegar
1/2 teaspoon sugar
1/4 teaspoon chili powder
1/4 teaspoon cumin
2 teaspoons fresh oregano (or 3/4 teaspoon dried oregano)

Method

Mix together all ingredients blending well.

Salad

1 can kidney beans
2 cups tomatoes, chopped
1/2 green pepper, chopped
1/2 red pepper, chopped
4 green onions, (scallions), sliced
1 cup diced jicama
salt and pepper to taste

Method

Combine salad ingredients with dressing in a medium sized bowl. Cover and refrigerate until serving time, stirring occasionally to blend flavors. To serve, drain salad with a slotted spoon and mound on lettuce leaves.

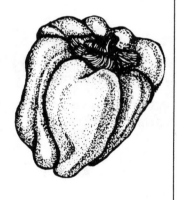

Nutrient Values:

Calories:	125	Cholesterol:	0 mg
Protein:	3.81 g	Fiber:	5.70 g
Carbohydrates:	20.2 g	% Fat Calories:	26
Total Fat:	3.76 g		

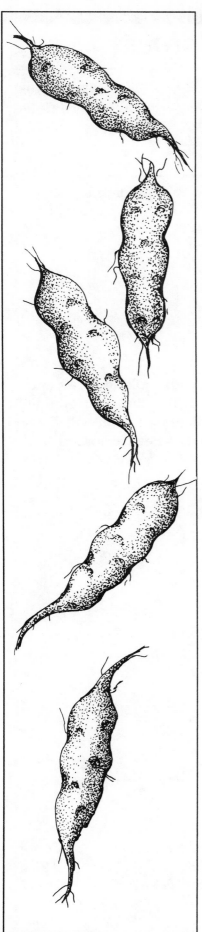

Sweet Potatoes and Yams

History: The sweet potato is a tuberous root of a tropical vine and is a member of the morning glory family. It is unrelated to the common potato. It arrived in Europe in the 16th century, and was brought to Britain by Sir Francis Drake, but they never became popular. They are popular in the United States, however, especially in the South. Yams are a darker, sweeter, more moist variety of the sweet potato.

Nutrition: Sweet potatoes are high in vitamin C and carotene.

Selecting: Look for firm, well-shaped potatoes with smooth skins. Avoid those with damp spots or cracks.

Storing: Keep in a dry, cool place. Do not refrigerate.

Candied Sweet Potatoes

These potatoes are very good with roast chicken or turkey. Watch them carefully towards the end of the cooking time — when there is little liquid in the pan.

Serves 8

6 medium-sized sweet potatoes, peeled and quartered
2 tablespoons butter
4 tablespoons brown sugar
4 tablespoons hot water
4 tablespoons dry white wine
1 1/2 tablespoons ground cinnamon
1/8 teaspoon salt

Method

Lightly spray a non-stick, 3 quart pan, with cooking spray, and saute the potatoes in the butter for about 10 minutes or until lightly browned. Add the remaining ingredients, and stir well. Cover the pan, and simmer until all the liquid has been absorbed, and the potatoes are tender — about 20 minutes. Serve hot.

Nutrient Values:

Calories:	179	Cholesterol:	7.77 mg
Protein:	1.59 g	Fiber:	3.77 g
Carbohydrates:	35.4 g	% Fat Calories:	17
Total Fat:	3.26 g		

Sweet Potatoes with Apples

This appetizing dish is a good source of vitamin C and fiber. It can be used any time of the year, but would be a good choice at holiday times, to replace the typical high calorie potato dishes that are usually served.

Serves 4

1 pound sweet potatoes
2 cooking apples
4 tablespoons seedless raisins
1 large lemon, the juice, and the grated rind
salt and pepper
2/3 cup chicken stock

Method

Pre-heat the oven to 350 degrees.

Peel, and thinly slice 1 pound of sweet potatoes. Peel, core and thickly slice the cooking apples.

In a small bowl, mix together the raisins, lemon juice, lemon rind, salt and pepper.

Lightly spray an 8 x 8 inch ovenproof dish with cooking spray. Make layers of the sweet potatoes, and apple slices, sprinkling each layer with the raisin mixture. Pour the chicken stock over the top.

Cover the dish, and bake for 40 - 50 minutes, or until the potatoes are tender. Serve hot.

Nutrient Values:

Calories:	1 9 8	Cholesterol:	0.166 mg
Protein:	2.83 g	Fiber:	5.49 g
Carbohydrates:	47.2 g	% Fat Calories:	4
Total Fat:	0.868 g		

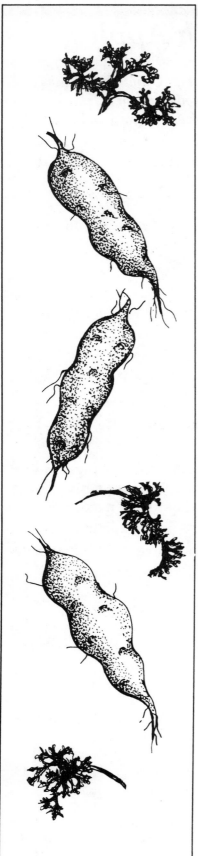

Baked Sweet Potatoes

This southern sweet potato recipe is low in fat, and easy to make. It is very good with chicken or turkey.

Serves 4

3 large sweet potatoes
3 tablespoons brown sugar
1 tablespoon unsalted butter
2 tablespoons water

Method

Cook the potatoes in their skins, in lightly salted water. When cool enough to handle, peel, and slice them lengthwise into three or four pieces.

Pre-heat the oven to 375 degrees.

Lightly spray an 8 x 8 inch, or similar sized deep baking dish with cooking spray. Put a layer of potatoes in the dish, sprinkle them with 1 tablespoon of sugar, and 2 teaspoons of butter cut into tiny pieces. Then make another layer of potatoes, sugar, and butter pieces; lastly, top with butter, and sprinkle with the remaining sugar.

Bake for about 20 minutes, and just before serving sprinkle with 2 tablespoons hot water.

Nutrient Values:

Calories:	184	Cholesterol:	7.77 mg
Protein:	1.53 g	Fiber:	3.40 g
Carbohydrates:	37.7 g	% Fat Calories:	16
Total Fat:	3.21 g		

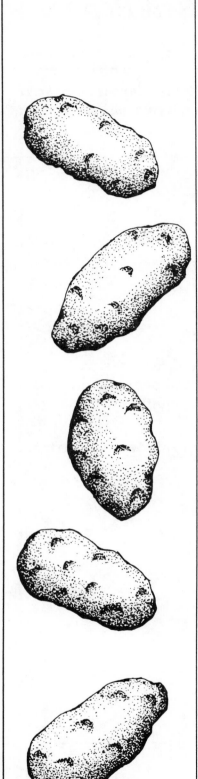

Potatoes

Potatoes which for some time went through a period of disgrace, have now been rehabilitated, and are no longer blamed for putting the extra inches on our waistlines. Most people now realize, that it is the butter and sour cream, that we garnish our potato with, that is the real culprit for putting on excess weight.

History: The potato was brought to Europe from Chile by Spanish conquerors in the latter part of the 16th century. More than 100 years passed before it became eaten in England; the Scots and Irish rejecting it initially because it was not mentioned in the Bible.

Nutrition: The potato is a source of protein, fiber, and a valuable source of vitamin C. Peeling a potato will greatly reduce its protein content, since the protein is highly concentrated just below the skin, and if a potato is boiled, as much as half of the vitamin C content is dissolved in the water. Green skin should be removed, however, as it contains a detrimental alkaloid.

Selecting: According to one survey, one potato in five is damaged, because of mechanical harvesting. Buying packaged potatoes is a mistake. Their bruises quickly turn black in the humid atmosphere inside the plastic bag, and the potatoes quickly go bad, and develop green, toxic skins as the result of the prolonged exposure to light. Idahoes are best for baking, White Rose, Shafters, or large red skins are best for boiling, mashing, and salads. The Majestic which grows well and keeps satisfactorily, has poor flavor, and tends to go black when boiled. Avoid potatoes with sprouts, or a greenish cast, which indicates long storage or over-exposure to light, and which will taste bitter. Look for well-shaped, firm potatoes, free of blemishes.

Storing: Keep in a cool, dry, dark place. Never refrigerate potatoes. Properly stored, potatoes will keep 2-3 weeks.

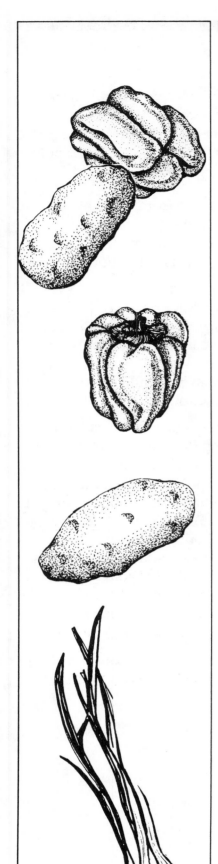

Potato Salad with Red Pepper and Scallions

This delicious potato salad needs no salt added to it, and is much lower in fat than regular potato salad. It is excellent served with cold chicken.

Serves 6

3 pounds potatoes
1/4 cup light mayonnaise
2 tablespoons yogurt
2 tablespoons Dijon mustard
freshly ground black pepper
1 bunch scallions, chopped
1 red pepper, cut into small pieces

Method

Cook the potatoes in their skins. Cool, and remove skins. Mix together mayonnaise, yogurt, mustard, and pepper. Add the scallions and red pepper, mix well. Add the slightly warm potatoes, and fold in gently.

Cover and refrigerate for at least 1 hour to allow flavors to macerate before serving.

Nutrient Values:

Calories:	245	Cholesterol:	2.50 mg
Protein:	5.35 g	Fiber:	4.24 g
Carbohydrates:	51.6 g	% Fat Calories:	9
Total Fat:	2.55 g		

Potatoes Stuffed with Bacon

These appetizing potatoes are not low in calories, and should be reserved for special occasions, or served for lunch with a salad. I find, however, that they fulfill my occasional desire for bacon, without consuming too much!

Serves 4

4 large baking potatoes
salt and pepper
4 slices bacon, broiled until crisp
8 ounces yogurt cheese (see page 40), or cottage cheese
3 tablespoons chopped, fresh chives, or scallions
1 tablespoon chopped, fresh parsley
4 tablespoons skim milk
4 ounces low-moisture, skim mozzarella

Method

Preheat oven to 400 degrees.

Scrub the potatoes, and score them down the middle lengthwise. Bake for 50-60 minutes or until cooked.

Cut the potatoes in half lengthwise, and very carefully scoop the potato out of the skin into a mixing bowl. Reserve the skins. Mash the potatoes by hand, add the well drained, crumbled bacon and season with salt and pepper.

In a separate bowl, mix together the yogurt cheese, or cottage cheese, chives or scallions, parsley, and enough milk to bind the ingredients; mix well.

Spoon the stuffing back into the reserved potato skins, and sprinkle the cheese over the top.

Return the potatoes back to the oven, and cook for 10-15 minutes or until the filling is slightly brown.

Nutrient Values:

Calories:	384	Cholesterol:	23.1 mg
Protein:	21.8 g	Fiber:	4.80 g
Carbohydrates:	54.3 g	% Fat Calories:	20
Total Fat:	8.60 g		

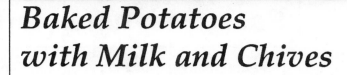

Baked Potatoes
with Milk and Chives

This recipe is adapted from a French version that uses heavy cream. It is very good with either fish or chicken.

Serves 4

4 large baking potatoes baked in their skins, and halved lengthwise
2 tablespoons unsalted butter
1/3 cup 2% low fat milk
2 tablespoons fresh chives, finely cut
salt and pepper to taste
4 tablespoons freshly grated Parmesan cheese

Method

Pre-heat the broiler.

Scoop out the pulp of the baked potato into a medium sized bowl. Reserve the potato skins. Break up the pulp, and add the butter, milk, chives, salt, and pepper. Beat until smooth. Refill the potato skins with this mixture, and sprinkle the cheese over the top. Broil for about 5 minutes, or until brown. Watch carefully or cheese will burn!

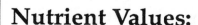

Nutrient Values:

Calories:	304	Cholesterol:	21.3 mg
Protein:	7.51 g	Fiber:	4.75 g
Carbohydrates:	52.2 g	% Fat Calories:	23
Total Fat:	7.87 g		

Brassicas

❖ Vegetables from the brassica genus (of the cruciferous family) or cabbage family may reduce the risk of cancer of the colon. According to the American Cancer Society something in these vegetables may help to block the formation of cancer in the body.

❖ Cruciferous vegetables include cabbage, broccoli, Brussels sprouts, rutabaga, collard, kale, turnip, kohlrabi, and cauliflower.

❖ Brassicas are high in vitamins and low in calories. For example 3 1/2 ounces of broccoli provide only 35 calories.

149

Brussels Sprouts

History: Brussels sprouts are grown mostly in California, although their origin was in Northern Europe around Brussels, Belgium.

Nutrition: Brussels sprouts are high in sulphur, hence their characteristic smell. They are a member of the brassica family, and a good source of fiber and vitamins A and C.

Yield: 1 pound Brussels sprouts, trimmed, will serve 5-6 people.

Selecting: Look for sprouts that are tight, firm, and green. Avoid large heads with yellow leaves.

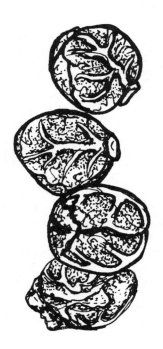

Storing: Do not wash brussels sprouts until ready to cook. Store in a plastic bag and refrigerate. Brussels sprouts should be used within a couple of days of purchasing, but I prefer to use them the same day that I buy them because their taste becomes stronger the longer they are stored.

Leftovers: Use brussels sprouts as an addition to stir-fry dishes.

Cut them into small pieces and add to salads.

Saute an onion in 1 tablespoon butter or diet margarine. Add cooked sprouts when the onion is almost cooked, just so they will heat through. Serve as a vegetable or use as a filling in an omelet.

Add to cooked fresh carrots, turnips or parsnips.

Cooking Hints: Prepare sprouts by removing any wilted leaves. Trim stems and cut an x in the bottom of the stem for even cooking. Steaming is the best method to prepare Brussels sprouts in order to preserve more vitamins and minerals. Overcooking creates a spongy, strong flavored mess. I often think that the reason so many people don't like Brussels sprouts is because they have not had fresh sprouts cooked properly. Sprouts should be crisp and delicately flavored.

Steamed Brussels sprouts with yogurt: Steam sprouts. Toss with a little non-fat yogurt, and some freshly ground black pepper.

Brussels sprouts with chestnuts: Melt 1 tablespoon diet margarine or butter for every 1 pound sprouts. Toss the warm steamed sprouts in the butter, and add 2 cups chestnuts, a little salt, and freshly ground black pepper.

Cabbage

History: Cabbage has been cultivated for over 4,000 years, making it one of the most ancient vegetables still grown. It grows in every kind of climate and is readily available all year.

Nutrition: Cabbage is high in vitamin C, potassium, and calcium. As with all brassicas, it is very important not to overcook the cabbage, or the vitamins and minerals will be lost.

Yield: 1 pound cabbage yields 5 firmly packed cups shredded cabbage raw, or 3 cups cooked. Two pounds cabbage yields about 9-10 cups sliced, or 5-6 cups cooked.

Selecting: Avoid cabbage that has leaves growing from the main stem below the head. These cabbages will have a strong flavor and coarse texture.

Storage: Sliced cabbage will keep 5-6 days refrigerated in a plastic bag that has been perforated. Whole cabbage will keep 1-2 weeks.

Cooking Hints: A couple of slices of stale bread in the cooking water will minimize the odor of cooking cabbage.

To prevent the color of red cabbage from fading try adding 1 tablespoon of vinegar or lemon juice to each 2 cups cooking water.

To remove cabbage leaves for stuffing: plunge the whole cabbage head into a pot of boiling water for 1 minute. Remove, drain and carefully pull off the leaves which will have softened.

Leftovers:

Bubble and squeak: This is a dish that is very popular in parts of England. Mix together equal amounts of cabbage and mashed potato and season well with a little salt and freshly ground black pepper. Cook in a little butter or diet margarine in a non-stick or stick resistant frying pan, pressing down to make it into a giant pancake. When it is brown on the bottom, reduce heat and cook until the pancake is heated through. Sauteed onion and/or ground meat can be added if desired.

Baked Cabbage with Chestnuts

Here's a great way to serve cabbage! This is a delicious dish that goes well with hot or cold meat, and provides fiber, and lots of vitamin C and A.

Serves 4

4 cups shredded green cabbage
1 cup nonfat yogurt
1/2 cup seedless dark raisins
1 cup roasted chestnuts
1/2 cup grated, sharp Cheddar cheese
grated nutmeg
salt and pepper

Method

Pre-heat oven to 375 degrees.

Put half of shredded cabbage in a 2 quart souffle dish, or similar sized ovenproof casserole or baking dish. Spread half of yogurt over cabbage. Sprinkle with raisins, chestnuts, salt and pepper. Put remaining cabbage over top of this layer and spread with remaining yogurt. Sprinkle grated cheese and a little grated nutmeg over the top.

Bake for 15-20 minutes, or until the top is lightly browned. Serve at once.

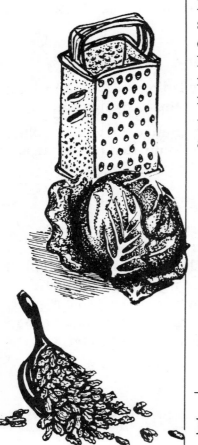

Nutrient Values:

Calories:	254	Cholesterol:	15.9 mg
Protein:	9.40 g	Fiber:	7.52 g
Carbohydrates:	43.6 g	% Fat Calories:	20
Total Fat:	5.79 g		

Cabbage Stuffed with Ham and Vegetables

This nutritious, high fiber recipe would easily be turned into a vegetarian dish by substituting carrots and celery for the ham.

Serves 4

2 pounds green cabbage, cored and kept whole
2 tablespoons butter
1/2 cup carrots, finely chopped
1/2 cup celery, finely chopped
1/2 cup onions, finely chopped
1/2 pound lean ham, thinly julienned
3 teaspoons garlic, chopped
1 cup thinly sliced onions
1 egg white
1/2 cup cooked, brown rice
freshly ground black pepper
1 teaspoon thyme
3 cups hot chicken or vegetable broth
1 can tomato paste
3-4 scallions

Method

Blanch the cabbage for 6 minutes. Cool slightly. Remove 12 well-shaped leaves. Shred the remaining cabbage. Melt 1 tablespoon butter in a stick resistant or non-stick pan that has been lightly sprayed with cooking spray. Saute the carrots, celery, onions, and 1 cup of shredded cabbage for about 8-10 minutes or until the cabbage is wilted. Do not allow cabbage to brown. Add 2-3 tablespoons stock if the pan gets too dry. Add the ham and garlic and cook 5 minutes longer. Set aside in a bowl to cool slightly.

Melt 1 tablespoon butter in the pan you have been using, and saute the sliced onions and the remaining shredded cabbage for about 5 minutes. Add to the ham and vegetable mixture.

Lightly spray a 13 x 9 x 2 inch baking dish. Beat the egg white and mix together with vegetable and ham mixture, brown rice, thyme, and pepper.

Place about 1 heaping tablespoon in the center of each leaf. Roll the leaf up, tucking in the open sides. Place in the baking dish, flap side down.

Mix the stock with the tomato paste and heat. Pour sauce over the cabbage rolls, cover with foil, and bake in a preheated 350 degree oven for about 40 minutes, basting from time to time. Serve with the pan juices.

Nutrient Values:

Calories:	315	Cholesterol:	42.9 mg
Protein:	21.9 g	Fiber:	9.74 g
Carbohydrates:	36.5 g	% Fat Calories:	29
Total Fat:	10.8 g		

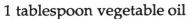

Red Cabbage with Apples and Raisins

This delicious salad is good as part of a buffet, or as an accompaniment to roast turkey or chicken.

Serves 8

1 tablespoon vegetable oil
1 large onion, thinly sliced
1 medium sized red cabbage, (2 pounds) coarsely shredded
4 ounces raisins
2 medium sized cooking apples
salt and pepper to taste
1/4 cup cider vinegar

Method

Heat the oil in a large non-stick frying pan. Cook the onions until soft, but not brown. Add the shredded cabbage and cover the pan. Cook for about 10 minutes over low heat, then add the raisins, apples, salt and pepper, add a little water; cook for another 10-12 minutes, then drain off any excess liquid. Add the vinegar, and adjust seasonings, mixing well. Cool before serving.

RAISINS

Nutrient Values:

Calories:	128	Cholesterol:	0 mg
Protein:	2.45 g	Fiber:	4.93 g
Carbohydrates:	27.9 g	% Fat Calories:	15
Total Fat:	2.29 g		

Red Cabbage Marinated with Pineapple and Blackberries

This unusual salad is low in calories and a good source of fiber. It can be used as a side salad, to accompany fish or meats, or as a light lunch.

Serves 8

4 cups red cabbage, shredded
1 cup carrots, grated
1 cup blackberries
1-8 ounce can pineapple tidbits, drained
2/3 cup unsweetened pineapple juice
1/4 cup red wine vinegar
1 tablespoon vegetable oil

Method

Combine cabbage, carrots, blackberries and pineapple pieces in a medium size bowl; cover, and set aside in the refrigerator for 20 minutes. Combine remaining ingredients in a small bowl, and stir well to mix. Pour over the cabbage mixture, and toss gently to coat. Cover and refrigerate for at least 4 hours, occasionally stirring and tossing gently to mix and distribute flavors.

Nutrient Values:

Calories:	66.5	Cholesterol:	0 mg
Protein:	0.942 g	Fiber:	2.79 g
Carbohydrates:	12.8 g	% Fat Calories:	24
Total Fat:	1.93 g		

Your Notes:

Broccoli Facts

History: Broccoli was brought to this country by Italian immigrants in 1920, and is now one of our most popular vegetables. It has been popular in several European countries for over 2,000 years.

Nutritional Information: Broccoli is a cruciferous vegetable, and people whose diets frequently include cruciferous vegetables have been shown to have lower risk of cancer, according to the American Cancer Society. Cabbage, cauliflower, brussels sprouts, rutabaga, kale, and turnips are other members of this family. Broccoli is also a wonderful source of vitamins A and C, and has fair amounts of riboflavin, iron, calcium and potassium. It is also a good source of fiber.

Selecting: Look for closely bunched green flowerets that are firm and have resilient stalks. Don't buy yellow flower buds and loosely bunched heads — this is a sign of age. Stalks that have open cores at the base will be tough and hollow.

Storing: Refrigerate unwashed in a plastic bag. Do not peel the stalks until you are ready to use them or they will become tough and dry.

Preparing: Wash well and cut of about 2 1/2 inches below the top of the flowerets. Peel the stalks, it is quite unbelievable how tender and tasty they are when peeled, and it completely changes the cooking time, the stems will be cooked in about the same time as the heads. The stems can be cut in slices and used in stir fries, with or without the heads and also julienned for a saute of mixed julienne vegetables.

157

Broccoli with Mustard Sauce

This mild tasting mustard sauce could also be used over baked fish or broiled chicken.

Serves 4

1 pound broccoli, washed, the stems cut off 2 1/2 inches below the top of the flowerets and then peeled and sliced into medium sized slices
2 teaspoons butter
1 tablespoon flour
1 cup skim milk
salt and pepper to taste
1 tablespoon Dijon style mustard
1/2 teaspoon lemon juice

Method

Steam the prepared broccoli until it is tender but still crisp, about 7 minutes.

Meanwhile prepare the sauce as follows: in a small saucepan melt the butter, and stirring constantly add the flour and cook for 1 minute. Add the milk gradually, whisking it briskly with a wire whisk until well blended. Stir in the salt, pepper and mustard cook over medium heat until the sauce begins to thicken. Add the lemon juice and stir well to combine. Pour over the steamed broccoli, and serve at once.

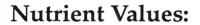

Nutrient Values:

Calories:	82.1	Cholesterol:	6.18 mg
Protein:	5.87 g	Fiber:	3.51 g
Carbohydrates:	11.1 g	% Fat Calories:	25
Total Fat:	2.54 g		

Broccoli with Tarragon and Fresh Red Pepper Sauce

The sauce in this recipe is very good, and can also be used over baked fish.

Serves 4

1 pound broccoli, washed, the stems cut off 2 1/2 inches below
    the flowerets and then peeled and cut into medium slices
2 red peppers, seeded, deribbed and sliced
1 medium onion, sliced thin
1 teaspoon garlic powder
1 cup chicken or vegetable stock
2 teaspoons white wine vinegar
1 tablespoon chopped tarragon or 1 teaspoon dried tarragon
1 teaspoon prepared horseradish
salt and freshly ground black pepper to taste

Method

Steam the broccoli until it is tender but still crisp, about seven minutes. Reserve the liquid used to steam the broccoli.

Prepare the red pepper sauce while the broccoli is steaming.

Red Pepper Sauce:

In a separate saucepan prepare to steam the red peppers and onions. Sprinkle them with the garlic powder and steam until tender. Put the red peppers and onions in a blender or food processor, adding the white wine vinegar, tarragon, horseradish, and salt and pepper. Puree. If the sauce is a little too thick, thin it out with some of the reserved liquid. Place the mixture in a medium saucepan just to re-heat, and serve over the broccoli.

Nutrient Values:

Calories:	67.5	Cholesterol:	0.250 mg
Protein:	5.62 g	Fiber:	5.02 g
Carbohydrates:	12.1 g	% Fat Calories:	12
Total Fat:	1.04 g		

Your Notes:

Cauliflower

History: Cauliflower has been cultivated since at least 600 B.C. it is native to the Mediterranean area, and came to England from France in the early 1600's. It was brought to America by the Colonists.

Nutrition: Cauliflower is a good source of vitamin C. It also provides potassium, plus other vitamins and minerals and is low in sodium.

Yield: 1 medium size head will serve 4 people.

Selecting: Look for clean, white or creamy-white heads with compact flowerets and fresh, green leaves. Avoid any heads that have brown spots.

Storage: Cauliflower does not keep well and should be used as soon as possible after buying. Refrigerate in a perforated plastic bag in the refrigerator when raw. Cauliflower needs oxygen, so don't store it in a sealed container.

Leftovers: Use any leftovers as soon as possible, as cauliflower looses its flavor quickly and becomes unappetizing.

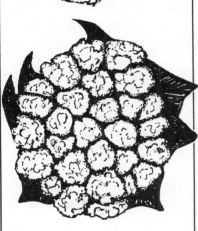

Cooking: There are few things worse then overcooked cauliflower; apart from creating a soggy, mushy, bad tasting mess, overcooking destroys the vitamins and minerals. Watch carefully, and only cook until barely tender.

Cauliflower puree with cheese: Puree with 1 tablespoon butter or diet margarine, top with a little Parmesan cheese and bake in a 350 degree oven.

Cauliflower and whipped potatoes: Add cauliflower to mashed potatoes with a little salt, and white pepper.

Cauliflower puree: Puree cauliflower; add seasonings to taste and heat gently. Add a little lite sour cream or nonfat yogurt.

Cauliflower with tomatoes and fresh basil: Heat together peeled, seeded, and chopped tomatoes. Add fresh basil. Gently fold into the cooked cauliflower flowerets. (The hot sauce will be sufficient to heat the flowerets).

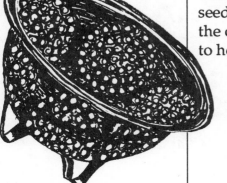

Cauliflower with Shallots

This tasty vegetable dish can be made very easily and quickly. The crumb mixture can be made ahead of time and reheated while you steam the cauliflower.

Serves 4

1 pound trimmed cauliflower flowerets
1 tablespoon butter or diet margarine
2 teaspoons chopped shallots
1/2 cup fresh whole wheat bread crumbs
1 hard cooked egg (white only), very finely chopped

Method

Steam cauliflower for 6-8 minutes until just tender.

While the cauliflower is steaming prepare the topping: Heat butter or margarine in a non-stick or stick resistant pan, and saute the shallots for 1 minute. Stir in the breadcrumbs, and cook until the crumbs are brown. Add the hard-cooked egg white and remove from heat. Place the cauliflower in a 2 quart serving dish, and sprinkle the topping over. Serve immediately while it is still hot.

Nutrient Values:

Calories:	66.7	Cholesterol:	5.18 mg
Protein:	3.69 g	Fiber:	3.02 g
Carbohydrates:	9.27 g	% Fat Calories:	29
Total Fat:	2.35 g		

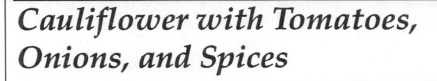

Cauliflower with Tomatoes, Onions, and Spices

The idea for this recipe came from Marian Morash's fabulous book "The Victory Garden" — one of my favorite cookbooks.

Serves 6

3/4 pound cauliflower flowerets
3/4 pound broccoli flowerets
2 teaspoons ground ginger
2 teaspoons ground cumin
1 teaspoon ground cardamom
1 teaspoon ground coriander
1/2 teaspoon tumeric
1/4 teaspoon cayenne pepper
1 teaspoon salt
1/4 teaspoon mustard seeds
3 cups pureed tomatoes
pinch sugar
1 tablespoon butter or diet margarine
1 cup onions, chopped
3 cups good flavored chicken stock
2 tablespoons chopped parsley

Method

Trim the cauliflowerets and steam for 5-6 minutes or until slightly undercooked. Trim the broccoli, and peel the stalks if using. Steam until tender. Meanwhile combine all of the spices, salt, and sugar. Heat the butter or margarine in a non-stick or stick resistant pan that has been lightly sprayed with cooking spray, and saute the chopped onions for about 10 minutes or until soft. Add the spices, tomatoes, and chicken stock. Simmer for 5 minutes or until sauce is slightly thickened. Add the cauliflower and broccoli, gently stirring for about 1 minute or until vegetables are cooked. Be cautious not to let the cauliflower become overcooked and mushy.

Nutrient Values:

Calories:	69	Cholesterol:	5.18 mg
Protein:	3.76 g	Fiber:	4.58 g
Carbohydrates:	10.5 g	% Fat Calories:	29
Total Fat:	2.57 g		

Beets, Carrots, and Turnips:
All vegetables with tops should
have their tops removed before
storing.

Beets

Nutrition: Beets are a good source of potassium.

Selecting: Beets are sold with or without their green tops. If you buy them with the tops on make sure the tops are fresh. Choose medium-sized, well-shaped globes with smooth, firm flesh and deep purple red color.

Storage: Beets will keep 2-3 weeks in the vegetable bin of the refrigerator.

Preparing: Beets can be baked, steamed, or boiled, and are a great vegetable to use in low fat cooking. Baking beets retains the flavor the best, but requires the longest time. Steaming takes less time, and not too much flavor is lost. Boiling beets is the least satisfactory. Not only are vitamins and minerals lost, but also color and flavor. Beets are done when their skins move slightly when pressed.

Cooking Hints: If you live in an area that has hard water add a little vinegar to the boiling water to prevent beets from fading. Beets bleed less if they are cooked in their skins, so be careful not to tear the skins when you wash them.

Beets

Beet Recipes

Baked Beets: Preheat oven to 300 degrees. Wash beets well, leaving skin on. Bake in an ovenproof pan for about 1 hour.

Baked Beets with onions: Preheat oven to 350 degrees. Peel and thinly slice 5 or 6 beets, and 1 onion. Layer in a small casserole that has been lightly sprayed with cooking spray. Add 1/3 cup hot chicken or vegetable stock, and season with salt and pepper. Cover and bake for 30-60 minutes, or until beets are done. (Serves 4)

Pickled Beets with Honey: Slice 4 cups cooked beets. Set aside. Heat 1 cup cider vinegar, 1 cup beet juice, and 2 tablespoons honey until it is well dissolved. Pour over beets, and when cool cover and refrigerate 6 hours or overnight before serving. Will keep for 1 week. (Makes 1 quart)

Steamed Beets: Carefully wash beets trying not to puncture skin. Put a small amount of water in a saucepan; bring to a boil. Place steamer rack in pan and add beets. Cover pan tightly and steam for 40-50 minutes depending on size of beets. Check once or twice during cooking to make sure water has not evaporated.

Beets with yogurt and herb dressing: Steam beets. Cool well. Toss with nonfat yogurt mixed with fresh herbs as a dressing.

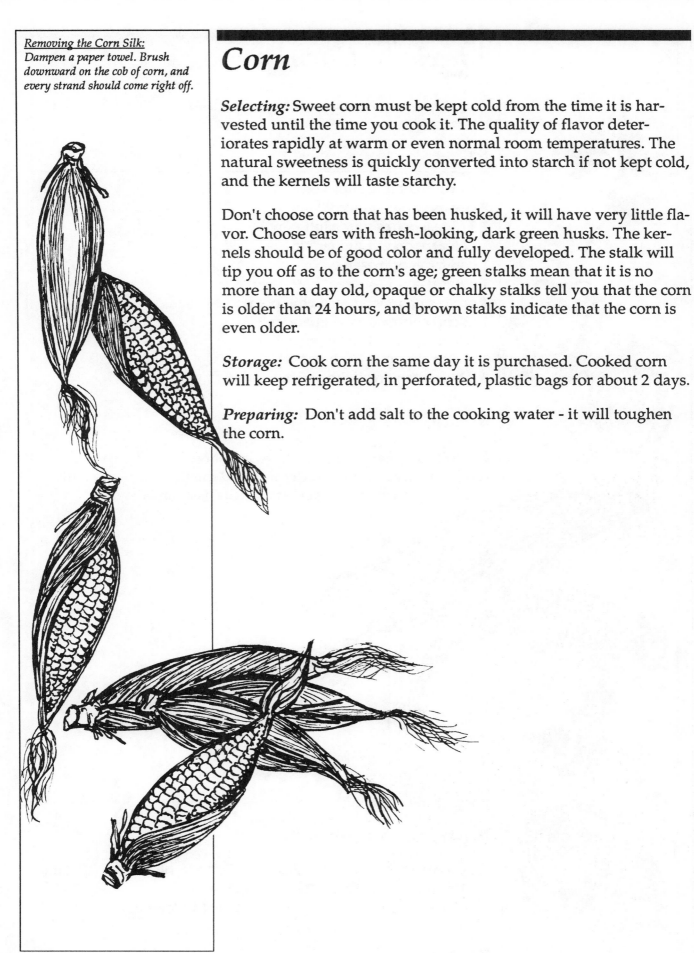

Removing the Corn Silk:
Dampen a paper towel. Brush downward on the cob of corn, and every strand should come right off.

Corn

Selecting: Sweet corn must be kept cold from the time it is harvested until the time you cook it. The quality of flavor deteriorates rapidly at warm or even normal room temperatures. The natural sweetness is quickly converted into starch if not kept cold, and the kernels will taste starchy.

Don't choose corn that has been husked, it will have very little flavor. Choose ears with fresh-looking, dark green husks. The kernels should be of good color and fully developed. The stalk will tip you off as to the corn's age; green stalks mean that it is no more than a day old, opaque or chalky stalks tell you that the corn is older than 24 hours, and brown stalks indicate that the corn is even older.

Storage: Cook corn the same day it is purchased. Cooked corn will keep refrigerated, in perforated, plastic bags for about 2 days.

Preparing: Don't add salt to the cooking water - it will toughen the corn.

167

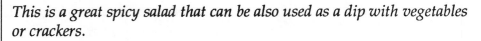

Mexican Corn

This is a great spicy salad that can be also used as a dip with vegetables or crackers.

Serves 4

1 medium onion, chopped
2 cloves garlic, minced
1 1/2 teaspoons mild chili powder
1/2 teaspoon ground cumin
1 cup fresh or frozen corn
1 cup salsa
4 ounces chopped green chili pepper
1/2 cup chopped green pepper
1/2 cup chopped red pepper
1/2 cup chopped fresh parsley
3 tablespoons fresh lime juice

Method

Combine all ingredients together in a large bowl. Cover and refrigerate overnight in order to blend the flavors. Serve with thinly sliced vegetables such as carrots, jicama, or squash.

Nutrient Values:

Calories:	72.0	Cholesterol:	0 mg
Protein:	2.30 g	Fiber:	3.49 g
Carbohydrates:	14.8 g	% Fat Calories:	17
Total Fat:	1.60 g		

The Onion Family

History: Onions go back to prehistoric times and originated in Asia. They have been revered as a food for centuries. The Spaniards brought them to North America, now the United States grows billions of pounds of onions each year.

Nutrition: Although onions have little nutritional value, they are known to stimulate the natural contractions of the intestine, and to improve the circulation of the blood. It has now been discovered that onions are an aid in reducing serum cholesterol, thus helping to lessen the likelihood of coronary heart disease.

Yield: 1 pound of onions yields 4 cups sliced, or 2 cups cooked. Serves 3-4.

Selecting:

Dry Onions: Choose onions that are clean and firm. The skins should be dry, smooth, and crackly. Onions with wet, soggy necks and soft or spongy bulbs with fresh sprouts indicate decay and should be avoided.

Green Onions: Select young and tender bunches with fresh green tops.

Leeks: Choose small or medium leeks for the most tender eating. Look for well-blanched bunches (white color extending 2" to 3" from bulb base).

Shallots: Buy dry, firm and well rounded bulbs.

Storage: Dry onions can be stored at room temperature or in the refrigerator, the important thing is to keep them dry. They will keep for 3 to 4 weeks. Green onions and Leeks should be kept in a plastic bag in the refrigerator and used as soon as possible. Shallots will keep up to 2 months, in a dry, well ventilated place.

Varieties:

Bermuda: Mild and sweet tasting. These onions are large and flatly shaped and usually golden in color. They are good raw or cooked.

Spanish: Jumbo and fawn-colored. Spanish onions are sweet and juicy. Serve them raw, stuffed or baked.

Yellow: Great for cooking, yellow onions have a pungent flavor. Round and golden, they're good chopped, sliced, diced, or fried.

Red or Italian: Robust in taste, and deep red to purple in color, slice them raw into salads. They add zest, color and tang.

White: Silver skinned, and small, white onions are best in stews, soups or creamed for side dishes.

Green or Spring: Good eaten raw with meat, cheese or fish. Chop the green tops and toss into a salad, cottage cheese or egg dishes. They're great stir-fried Chinese style.

Shallots: Delicate tasting cousin of the onion and garlic. The reddish-brown skinned bulb is divided into cloves like garlic. Shallots are a subtle, yet tangy flavoring agent.

Leeks: More nutritious than other onions, leeks have more carotene, vitamin C and minerals. A mild tasting member of the onion family, leeks look like giant spring onions. Leeks usually have to be well trimmed — 2 pounds will yield about 1 pound cleaned. They add a unique flavor to soups and stews.

Braised Onions

This is a good vegetable to serve with many chicken or fish dishes. Sliced onion rings or small frozen onions can be prepared very quickly. Leftovers can be used to enhance many other recipes.

Serves 6

1 teaspoon safflower oil
1 pound small, peeled onions, fresh or frozen
1/2 cup chicken or vegetable stock
2 sprigs parsley
salt and pepper to taste

Method

Cut an x in the root end of each onion so that they will cook more evenly and remain whole.

In a non-stick pan, heat the oil, and add the onions. Saute for 3-4 minutes or until lightly browned, (if using frozen onions they will not brown). Add the remaining ingredients and bring the liquid to a boil. Cover the pan, reduce the heat, and simmer for 15-20 minutes until onions are tender.

Nutrient Values:

Calories:	31.5	Cholesterol:	0.083 mg
Protein:	0.975 g	Fiber:	0.921 g
Carbohydrates:	5.23 g	% Fat Calories:	25
Total Fat:	0.914 g		

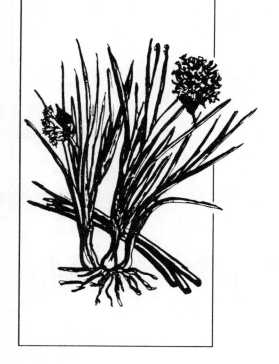

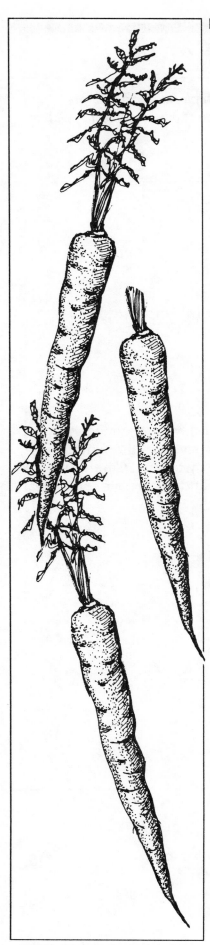

Carrots

History: The ancient Greeks used carrots for medicine. Carrots were brought by the Dutch to England, and to the United States by the early colonists.

Nutrition: Carrots are rich in beta-carotene, a compound that converts to vitamin A in the body. Scientists believe that vitamin A may be an agent that can reduce the tendency for malignant cells to multiply. Choose deeply colored carrots, they contain more carotene than the paler ones.

Yield: 1 pound carrots = 3 1/2 cups - 4 cups, or 3-4 servings.

Selecting: Choose firm, well-shaped, fresh-looking carrots. "Cliptops" are best, because the tops draw moisture from the carrots. Black stem ends indicate that the carrots are old.

Storage: Remove tops if attached. Place in a plastic bag and refrigerate. They will keep 2-3 weeks. Cooked carrots keep 2-3 days refrigerated.

Cooking Hints: Baking or steaming are the best ways to prepare carrots, in order to preserve the maximum amount of vitamins and minerals, and use the least amount of fat. Here are some suggestions:

Blanched or steamed:

Mashed: Mash 1 pound steamed carrots. Combine with 1 tablespoon butter or diet margarine, salt, and white pepper. Re-heat before serving. Add a little non-fat yogurt if you like. Serves 3-4.

With Mashed Potato: Combine 1 pound mashed carrots, 1 pound mashed potatoes, 5 tablespoons nonfat yogurt, salt, pepper, and a large pinch of nutmeg. Serves 6.

With Honey: Steam 1 pound carrots. Sprinkle with a little salt and pepper; toss in pan with 2-3 tablespoons honey. Sprinkle with 1 tablespoon chopped fresh parsley and serve. Serves 3-4.

With Fresh Herbs and Yogurt: Steam 1 pound carrots. Roll each carrot in 2-3 tablespoons nonfat yogurt and sprinkle with 2-3 tablespoons of chopped fresh chives, dill, basil or rosemary. Serves 3-4.

With Peas: Steam separately. Toss together and add 1 tablespoon of diet margarine or sprinkle with Molly McButter.

Leftovers:

Use pureed carrots to thicken sauces. Freeze in tiny containers or ice-cube trays so that you have them for this purpose.

Mash and reheat. Add herbs or cinnamon, about 1 teaspoon per pound carrots.

Carrot and Raisin Salad

This salad is loaded with raisins and pineapple, and is one of my favorites. You may want to reduce the amount of pineapple, depending upon your own personal taste.

Serves 6

2 pounds grated carrots
1 cup dark raisins
2 tablespoons lite mayonnaise
1/2 cup nonfat yogurt
2 tablespoons lemon juice
2 teaspoons sugar
2 - 8 ounce cans pineapple, drained, or 10 ounces fresh
     pineapple, cut into chunks
salt and pepper to taste.

Method

In a large bowl mix together mayonnaise, yogurt, vinegar, sugar, salt and pepper. Toss the carrots and raisins together with the dressing in the bowl. Check seasoning by tasting. Carefully add more sugar or salt as necessary. Cover and refrigerate for several hours before serving.

Nutrient Values:

Calories:	201	Cholesterol:	1.54 mg
Protein:	3.74 g	Fiber:	7.19 g
Carbohydrates:	47.5 g	% Fat Calories:	7
Total Fat:	1.63 g		

Carrot Salad with Mustard and Horseradish

This savory salad goes well with cold meats.

Serves 4

1 pound grated carrots
1/2 cup nonfat yogurt
4 tablespoons lite mayonnaise
1 tablespoon horseradish
1 tablespoon Dijon mustard
1 teaspoon sugar
salt and pepper to taste
1 tablespoon chopped parsley

Method

Combine all ingredients except the carrots and parsley in a medium sized bowl. Add the grated carrots. Taste, and adjust seasonings. Cover, refrigerate and let marinate for several hours. Before serving, sprinkle with chopped parsley.

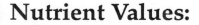

Nutrient Values:

Calories:	109	Cholesterol:	4.13 mg
Protein:	3.07 g	Fiber:	3.73 g
Carbohydrates:	17.8 g	% Fat Calories:	26
Total Fat:	3.32 g		

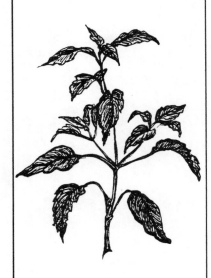

Vegetable Lasagne with Fresh Herbs

This wonderful, fresh-tasting vegetable lasagna, is greatly enhanced by using fresh herbs. Peeling the broccoli produces pale, tender-fleshed stalks that can also be used in stir-fries, or steamed and then topped with a little freshly grated Parmesan cheese. Don't peel the stalks until just before you plan to use them though; they will dry out and become tough.

Serves 6 (2 rolls each)

For the Tomato Sauce:

1 tablespoon safflower oil
1 medium onion, chopped
2 carrots, peeled and chopped
2 celery stalks, trimmed and chopped
3 garlic cloves, sliced thin
4 tablespoons chopped fresh basil, (or 4 teaspoons dried basil)
freshly ground black pepper
2/3 cup ruby red port, or 2/3 cup good quality beef stock
28 ounce can unsalted tomatoes, drained and chopped
3 level tablespoons tomato paste
1/2 cup unsweetened applesauce

For the Lasagna Rolls:

12 lasagnas
10 ounces yogurt cheese (see page 40)
8 ounces low fat 2% cottage cheese
1 cup broccoli stalks, peeled, chopped, and then steamed for 5 minutes
1 cup fresh mushrooms, sliced
3 scallions, (the white and green part), chopped
3 tablespoons chopped fresh basil (or 3 teaspoons dried)
2 tablespoons chopped fresh oregano, (or 2 teaspoons dried)
1/4 cup chopped fresh parsley

Method

To make the sauce:

Heat the oil in a large nonstick pan. Add the onion, carrot, and celery, and saute for 2 minutes stirring frequently. Add the garlic, and saute for another minute. Stir in the basil, pepper, and port or beef stock. Boil the liquid until it is reduced by half, which will take about 2-3 minutes. Add the tomatoes, tomato paste and the applesauce. Bring to a boil, and then reduce the heat to low. Simmer the sauce gently for 30-35 minutes. Puree the sauce in a food processor or blender and then return it to the saucepan. Set the pan aside.

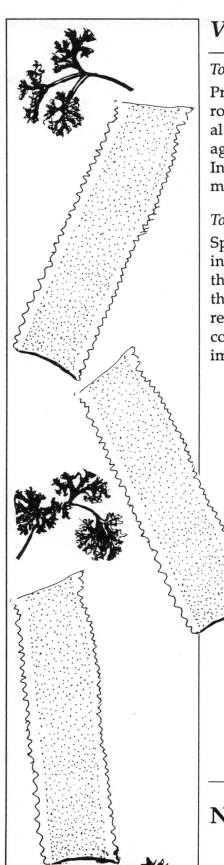

Vegetable Lasagne with Fresh Herbs *(cont'd)*

To make the lasagna roll-ups:

Preheat the oven to 350 degrees. Bring 4 quarts of water to a rolling boil. Add the lasagna with 2 teaspoons salt. Cook until al dente, which will take about 12 minutes if you are using packaged lasagna. Drain and spread on a clean dish towel to dry. In a large bowl, mix the yogurt cheese, cottage cheese, broccoli, mushrooms, scallions, basil, oregano, and parsley.

To assemble the lasagna rolls:

Spread 1 cup of the tomato sauce over the bottom of an 11 x 13 inch baking dish. Divide the cheese-vegetable mixture between the lasagne strips, and starting at one end, roll up the strip. Place the roll with the seam side down in the dish. Repeat with the remaining strips. Pour the rest of the sauce over the rolls, and cover the baking dish with foil. Bake for 15-20 minutes, and serve immediately with a tossed salad.

Nutrient Values:

Calories:	375	Cholesterol:	16.5 mg
Protein:	24.1 g	Fiber:	5.86 g
Carbohydrates:	48.4 g	% Fat Calories:	19
Total Fat:	7.37 g		

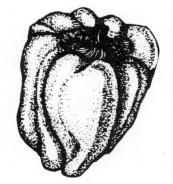

Vegetarian Stuffed Peppers

Two of these peppers would make a low calorie main meal, or serve as a vegetable with chicken or fish.

Serves 4 as a vegetable, or 2 as a main meal

For the sauce:

2 cups tomato sauce
1 tablespoon tomato paste
1/3 cup applesauce
1/2 cup red wine
1 small onion, chopped
2 cloves garlic, pressed
1 tablespoon fresh oregano, (or 1 teaspoon dried)
1 tablespoon fresh basil, (or 1 teaspoon dried)

Method

Combine all ingredients in a medium saucepan, and simmer for 45 minutes.

For the stuffing:

2 cups cooked brown rice
1 cup chopped zucchini
1 small onion, chopped
1 cup mushrooms, sliced thin
1 cup low fat cottage cheese
2 cups fresh spinach, chopped

4 bell peppers

Method

Combine all stuffing ingredients, and stuff into peppers. Cover peppers and bake at 350 degrees for 1 hour. Serve with the sauce.

Nutrient Values:

Calories:	317	Cholesterol:	4.75 mg
Protein:	17.3 g	Fiber:	9.50 g
Carbohydrates:	55.6 g	% Fat Calories:	8
Total Fat:	2.70 g		

Eggplant

Selecting: Eggplant should be firm, heavy in relation to size with a dark, rich purple-black color. Choose those that are not wilted, shriveled, soft or flabby, and which are free from brown scars or cuts.

Storage: Do not keep eggplant too cold. Use them within 2 or 3 days or they will become bitter and develop soft brown spots.

Preparation: Be sure to lightly salt the eggplant before cooking it in order to draw out the bitter juices which the eggplant will otherwise exude as it cooks. After salting, place in a colander for 30 minutes or more. Lightly squeeze out moisture, and pat dry. Salted and drained eggplant uses about 1/4 the amount of oil used with unsalted eggplant. That's a lot less oil! However, steaming is the best method to use in lowfat cooking.

Nutritional Information: Eggplant is low in sodium, and a good source of fiber.

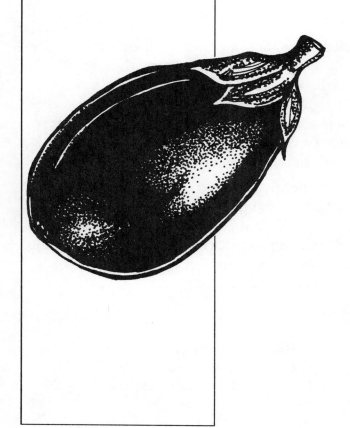

Ratatouille

Vegetarians in Asia have relied for centuries upon eggplant as a meat substitute. Some cooks like to peel it before cooking, and others enjoy eating it unpeeled. Either way, the following recipe is one that I make frequently. It keeps well, covered, and refrigerated, and can be used one day as a main meal, and the next day as a vegetable.

Serves 6

1 medium eggplant, cut into large slices, lightly salted, drained, patted dry, and then cut into large cubes
4 teaspoons olive oil
2 medium onions, sliced
2 cloves garlic, crushed
3 zucchini, sliced
1 red pepper, cored, seeded, and sliced
1 green pepper, cored, seeded, and sliced
3 tomatoes, peeled, seeded, and sliced, or 6 small canned tomatoes, including juice
1 teaspoon ground coriander
4 tablespoons fresh basil (or 1 tablespoon dry)
bouquet garni*
salt and pepper
extra chicken stock

Method

Preheat the oven to 350 degrees. In a large, nonstick, ovenproof casserole that has been lightly sprayed with cooking spray, heat the oil. Saute the onions and garlic, until the onion is soft but not brown. Add the zucchini and peppers and cook for 1 minute. (If the casserole becomes too dry, add a few tablespoons of water or chicken stock, and cover the casserole for a couple of minutes in order to create steam. Remove cover and continue to saute). Set aside.

Steam the eggplant until slightly soft, and then add it to the other vegetables. Add the tomatoes and their juice, coriander, basil and bouquet garni. Season with salt and pepper. Bake covered for 25-30 minutes. This is delicious served as a meatless meal, as a filling for an omelet, or as a vegetable with fish, or chicken.

Nutrient Values:

Calories:	108	Cholesterol:	0 mg
Protein:	4.00 g	Fiber:	6.36 g
Carbohydrates:	17.9 g	% Fat Calories:	27
Total Fat:	3.69 g		

Leeks

History: Leeks were known in Egypt and other Mediterranean countries before Biblical times. They had reached Wales by 640 A.D. and became the Welsh national emblem. The colonists brought leeks to America, where for some reason they didn't become as popular as they were in Europe. I was quite surprised when I came to the U.S. to find that leeks were relegated to exotic vegetable status and sold at a high price.

Nutrition: Leeks are much more nutritious than other members of the onion family, and contain more carotene, vitamin C and minerals.

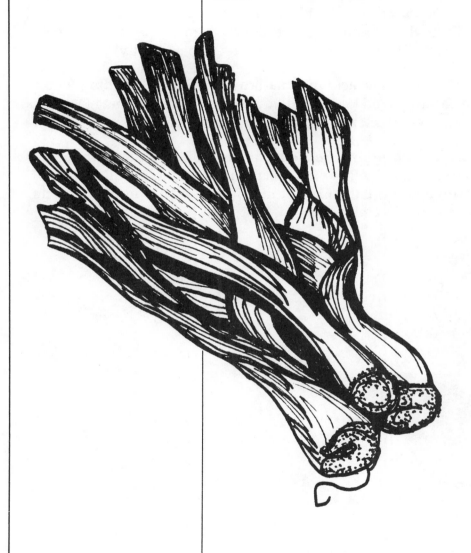

Tomatoes

The lowly supermarket tomato is a very distant relative of the real thing! Your best choices (apart from growing your own) are those labeled "greenhouse" or "hot house". These tomatoes are picked when almost ripe, and have more flavor than out of season tomatoes. Canned tomatoes for cooking are a better choice than the flavorless, dry specimens that we have come to accept most of the year.

Storing: Do not refrigerate tomatoes unless absolutely necessary. Temperatures below 55 degrees prevent ripening, and over 80 degrees will cause tomatoes to spoil quickly. Too much sunlight will cause tomatoes to soften without fully ripening. Ripe tomatoes should be used within 3 days. Freezing fresh tomatoes changes the taste and texture, although many people still do it. Cooked fresh tomatoes however, freeze beautifully.

Watchpoint: The acid in tomatoes reacts with aluminum (except for the anodized kind), and you end up with a strange taste. Cook in stainless steel, teflon coated, or enamel pans.

Nutritional Information: One medium sized tomato (about 5 ounces) supplies 3/4 of the recommended dietary allowance of vitamin C, more than 1/4 of the vitamin A plus iron and niacin. All for only 35 calories!

To peel tomatoes:
bring a pot of water to the boil,
turn off the heat, and place the
tomatoes in the boiling water for 1
or 2 minutes. Remove tomatoes
with a slotted spoon, and pierce the
center top of each with a sharp
knife. The peel will come off easily .

Leek and Tomato Casserole

This vegetable dish is loaded with vitamins and minerals and is good served hot or cold. It is also quick and easy to prepare — an added bonus!

Serves 4

4 cups leeks, thoroughly washed and sliced
8 medium-sized tomatoes, peeled (optional) and sliced, or 8 canned tomatoes, crushed
1 lemon
salt and pepper
1 large garlic clove, crushed

Method

Preheat oven to 350 degrees.

Lightly spray a 1 1-2 quart oven-proof dish with cooking spray. Put half of the leeks into the dish and cover with tomatoes. Sprinkle with a little salt, black pepper, juice from half of the lemon, and crushed garlic clove. Top with remaining leeks, rest of lemon juice and a little more salt and pepper.

Cover and bake for 50-60 minutes, or until the leeks are just tender.

Nutrient Values:

Calories:	11 4	Cholesterol:	0 mg
Protein:	3.82 g	Fiber:	6.09 g
Carbohydrates:	26.3 g	% Fat Calories:	6
Total Fat:	0.858 g		

Broiled Tomatoes Parmesan

Make these in the summer when the tomatoes are large, juicy, and full of flavor.

Serves 6

2 tablespoons nonfat yogurt
2 tablespoons light mayonnaise
1/4 cup grated Parmesan cheese
1/4 cup minced green onions, white part only
2 tablespoons minced parsley
3 medium sized firm tomatoes, cut in half

Method

Preheat broiler.

Combine all ingredients except tomatoes in a small bowl and mix well. Very carefully spread mixture on the tomatoes, about 1/4 inch thick.

Broil 4 inches from heat for about 2-3 minutes or until lightly browned. Serve immediately.

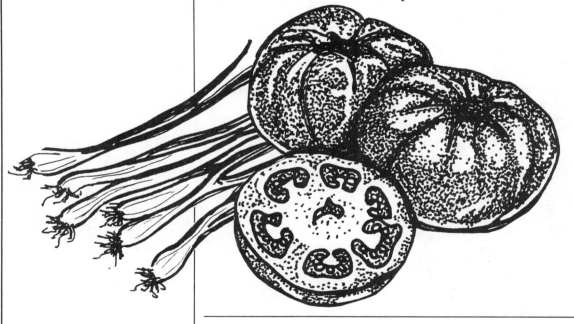

Nutrient Values:

Calories:	41.4	Cholesterol:	2.69 mg
Protein:	2.37 g	Fiber:	1.49 g
Carbohydrates:	5.52 g	% Fat Calories:	30
Total Fat:	1.47 g		

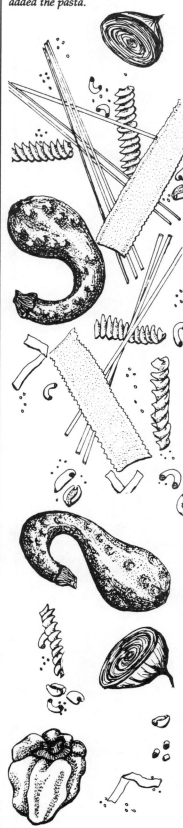

To cook pasta:
For evenly cooked pasta, immerse it gradually into water that is furiously boiling, so the temperature of the water is not disturbed too much. Add the salt after you have added the pasta.

Pasta Primavera

This colorful pasta dish is great for lunch or dinner. Use only the freshest of vegetables, which can be varied according to the season.

Serves 4

---

8 ounces dried spaghetti or fettucine or 12 ounces fresh
2 medium tomatoes, peeled, seeded and coarsely chopped. Use canned if necessary
1 tablespoon olive oil
1 small onion, finely chopped
1/4 teaspoon red pepper flakes
1/2 pound mushrooms thinly sliced
2 cloves garlic, minced
1 cup asparagus or green beans, cut diagonally
1 cup cauliflower
1 medium sized yellow squash, thinly sliced
1 medium sized red or green pepper, peeled and cut into thin strips
1/2 cup fresh or frozen peas
salt and freshly ground black pepper to taste
3 tablespoons freshly chopped parsley
1/4 cup Parmesan cheese

Method

Start to heat pasta cooking water in a large pot. Time pasta so it is cooked when the sauce is finished. Make sure the water is at a rolling boil before putting the pasta in the water, then add the salt, and lastly the pasta.

Heat olive oil in a large non-stick or stick resistant skillet. Saute onion and red pepper flakes for 3-4 minutes. Add mushrooms and garlic. Cook for 2 minutes over medium high heat. Add the asparagus pieces, cauliflower, yellow squash, and peppers. Cook, covered, for 2 minutes. Add the tomatoes, peas, salt and pepper. Cook for 2-3 minutes. Toss with hot, well drained pasta. Top with parsley and Parmesan cheese. Serve immediately on warm plates.

Nutrient Values:

Calories:	193	Cholesterol:	3.93 mg
Protein:	10.5 g	Fiber:	6.75 g
Carbohydrates:	34.8 g	% Fat Calories:	12
Total Fat:	2.74 g		

Rice

History: Although India was probably the birthplace of rice, the first clear evidence of it's cultivation comes from China in about 3000 B.C. During the 4,000 years of Imperial China, the Chinese Emperors and other members of the hierarchy took part in an annual symbolic ceremony of plowing a rice field. The Arabs introduced rice to Spain, and it spread to Italy in the 15th century. In 1700, rice finally reached South Carolina where it was first cultivated, and this became the most important growing region in America for a long time.

Nutritional Information: Brown rice, which is a good source of fiber and vitamins and minerals, is the grain with only the husk removed. Almost all minerals in brown rice are lost in the manufacturing of white rice, the most serious loss being thiamine. A lack of vitamin thiamine leads to the deficiency disease beriberi. The loss of thiamine in milled rice is minimized by a process called parboiling. This method steeps the unmilled rice in warm water for several days, it is then steam heated and finally dried. The thiamine and other valuable vitamins and minerals that are contained in the husk and bran, dissolve in the warm water and are carried into the endosperm which makes up three-quarters of the grain. Rice treated this way contains more than twice the thiamine as untreated milled rice.

Rice Variations: Add chopped mushrooms, celery, onion, green or red pepper to the rice at the beginning of the cooking time. Replace part of the water with chicken stock, white wine or fruit juice. Before removing rice from saucepan, toss in some freshly chopped herbs.

Fried Rice

Fried rice is not only a wonderful way to use up leftover rice, but also an opportunity to create a delicious feast with any leftover meat or vegetables you may have. Use brown rice for optimum nutrition.

Serves 6

2 egg whites and 1 egg yolk
2 teaspoons water
salt and pepper
1 tablespoon vegetable oil
1 large onion, chopped
4 ounces lean cooked chopped ham
4 cups cold cooked rice
1/3 cup cooked peas
4 scallions (green onions), chopped, including green part
1 tablespoon low-sodium soy sauce

Method

In a small bowl mix together the egg whites, yolk, and water. Season with salt and pepper. Heat one teaspoon oil in a wok or large, heavy frying pan. Pour in the egg mixture and cook as scrambled eggs. Set aside.

Add the remaining oil to the pan, and saute the onion until soft. Add the chopped ham, rice, peas and scallions, and cook stirring constantly for two minutes. Add the egg and soy sauce, and cook for 1 minute more. Serve immediately.

Variations: Any cooked meat or leftover vegetables can be used.

Nutrient Values:

Calories:	245	Cholesterol:	55.9 mg
Protein:	9.87 g	Fiber:	3.75 g
Carbohydrates:	39.7 g	% Fat Calories:	19
Total Fat:	5.17 g		

Brown Rice with Herbs

This recipe goes well with many of the dishes in this book. Since brown rice takes so long to cook, consider making up a double batch each time you cook it, and use it later in the week.

Serves 6

1 cup brown rice
1 1/2 cups defatted chicken stock
3/4 cup water
1 teaspoon low-sodium soy sauce
1/2 teaspoon garlic powder
1/4 teaspoon dried rosemary, crushed
1/4 cup chopped pimento
2 teaspoons fresh lemon juice

Method

In a medium saucepan combine all ingredients except pimento and lemon juice. Bring to a boil, cover, and reduce heat to a simmer. Cook covered for 40-50 minutes or until all water is absorbed. Add the lemon juice and pimento and mix well.

Nutrient Values:

Calories:	124	Cholesterol:	0.250 mg
Protein:	3.68 g	Fiber:	1.14 g
Carbohydrates:	24.9 g	% Fat Calories:	7
Total Fat:	0.969 g		

Persian Rice with Herbs

This dish is a delicious accompaniment to fish. It is traditionally served on New Year's in Iran, because its greenness is believed to ensure happiness in the year ahead.

Serves 4

1 1/4 cups Basmati or long-grain rice
1 tablespoon chopped fresh chives or 1 teaspoon dried chives
1 tablespoon chopped fresh parsley
2 tablespoons chopped mixed fresh herbs (or 2 teaspoons dried herbs such as tarragon, thyme, basil, or marjoram)
grated rind of 1/2 lemon
salt and freshly ground black pepper to taste

Method

Put the Basmati or rice into a medium saucepan. Cover with 2 1/2 cups of water and bring to a boil. Lower the heat and simmer for 5 minutes.

Add chives, parsley, mixed fresh herbs, grated lemon rind, salt and pepper. Mix well with the rice, cover the pan and simmer gently for about 10 minutes or until the rice is tender and the water has been absorbed.

Nutrient Values:

Calories:	211	Cholesterol:	0 mg
Protein:	3.96 g	Fiber:	0.921 g
Carbohydrates:	46.9 g	% Fat Calories:	1
Total Fat:	0.246 g		

Fish and Poultry

For the health-conscious cook, fish and poultry are low in fat, and have the added benefit of being fast and easy to prepare. It is important not to overcook fish, as this dries it out; perfectly cooked fish is opaque, and flakes slightly. Buy fresh fish whenever possible, it should only smell mildly fishy, if it has a stronger odor don't buy it. Frozen fish can also be used, but defrost it in the refrigerator, not on the kitchen counter, since the inside portions can remain frozen, while the outside can deteriorate.

Remove the excess fat and skin from chicken before cooking; there is a 20% transference of fat from chicken skin to the meat during cooking.

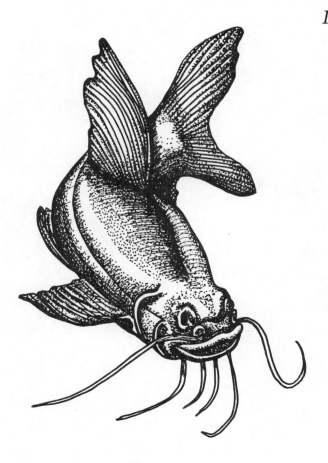

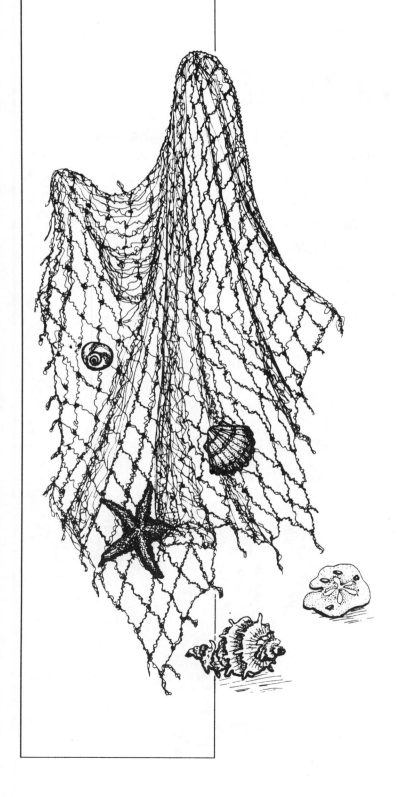

Poultry and Fish

Poultry Facts

History: Present day chickens are descended from the jungle of Southeast Asia and appear to date back to 2500 B.C. They were usually reserved as a luxury however, since it took months to raise a bird to its maturity, and hens were prized for their eggs.

Nutrition: Chicken is an excellent source of protein, niacin, calcium, minerals, vitamin A and riboflavin. It is easy to digest and lower in calories and fats than most other meats. To keep the fat at a minimum, remove the skin and any visible fat from the chicken pieces before cooking. Whole chickens need to be cooked with skin on or they will dry out, so remove skin before eating. Chicken with the skin has 53 percent fat calories, while chicken without the skin has 31 percent fat calories. Frying chicken adds even more fat.

Selecting Poultry: Birds of the highest quality have a shield-shaped label stating that they are USDA "Grade A". The age of the bird, which will determine its tenderness, is often indicated. Older birds are more flavorful, but are less tender, and should be tenderized by braising or simmering in liquid. Young poultry has tender meat, and can be barbecued, fried, broiled, or roasted.

Skin color is not an indication of quality. It may vary from white to yellow according to whatever the bird was fed.

Storing: Unwrap the poultry from the meat market wrapping, place it on a platter, and cover it loosely with plastic wrap before refrigerating. Frozen unstuffed poultry should be kept in the freezer.

Thawing Poultry: Thaw poultry gradually in the refrigerator whenever possible, as poultry goes bad at room temperature quite quickly. The cold water method can be used however, if you are in a hurry.

Cold water method: Place the poultry in the original plastic wrap in the sink or a large bowl, and cover with cold water. Be sure to change the water regularly until the meat thaws. It will take about 1 hour for a small game hen to thaw, 2 hours for a 3 to 4 pound bird, a 12 to 20 pound turkey will take 6 to 8 hours to thaw.

Refrigerator method: Place the bird, in its original wrap, on a plate in the refrigerator. A 2 to 4 pound bird will take 12 to 24 hours.

Storing Cooked Poultry: Do not allow cooked poultry to stand at room temperature for more than 1 1/2 hours after cooking. Loosely wrap meat in foil, or plastic wrap, and use within 2 to 3 days. Gravy and stuffing should be stored separately. Always remove stuffing from the cavity of the bird before refrigerating, as serious illness can result if the stuffing is not removed.

To freeze the cooked poultry, cool and separate the meat from the stuffing and gravy, before freezing separately. Poultry keeps frozen for about 2 months, but the stuffing and gravy should be used within 3 to 4 weeks.

If you find that you have dried lemons on hand, drop them in boiling water, remove pan from the heat, and allow to stand for about 5 minutes. Dry the lemons and then squeeze, they will yield plenty of juice.

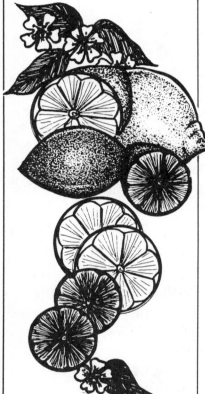

Lemon Chicken

This easy to prepare dish is good either hot or cold. Try it next time you have a picnic, or try it when you have to cook for a crowd — but don't leave out the overnight marinating, or the wonderful lemony flavor won't be there!

Serves 4

1 tablespoon safflower oil
4 whole chicken breasts, skinned, and boned
1 1/4 cups fresh lemon juice (about 5 lemons)
1/3 cup unbleached flour
salt & pepper to taste
1 teaspoon arrowroot
1 1/2 teaspoons Hungarian paprika
1/2 cup defatted chicken stock
1 tablespoon brown sugar
1 small lemon thinly sliced
1/2 teaspoon fines herbes, (or a mixture of sweet herbs to make 1/2 teaspoon)

Method

The evening before cooking the chicken, place the chicken pieces in a shallow baking dish and pour the lemon juice over the chicken to marinate. Turn occasionally.

Preheat the oven to 375 degrees. Remove chicken from the lemon juice, reserving the lemon juice. On a flat dish, combine the flour, paprika, salt and pepper, and coat the chicken with mixture. Bake for 25 minutes turning once.

Reserve 1/4 cup of lemon juice, and mix together with the arrowroot in a small bowl. Whisk the remaining lemon juice, stock, brown sugar and fines herbes together in a small saucepan, and heat until almost boiling. Add the arrowroot mixture and bring to a boil stirring constantly. Pour the thickened sauce over the chicken, and bake for 25 minutes more, basting frequently, chicken is done when juices run clear when pricked with a fork. Serve hot or cold.

Nutrient Values:

Calories:	235	Cholesterol:	68.1 mg
Protein:	29.2 g	Fiber:	0.712 g
Carbohydrates:	18.4 g	% Fat Calories:	21
Total Fat:	5.47 g		

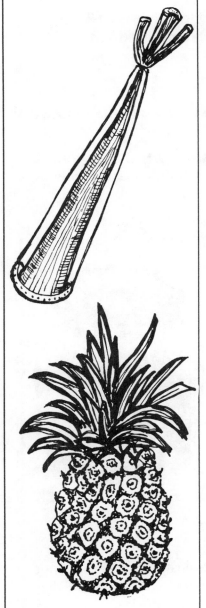

Chicken Salad with Pineapple

This salad looks very pretty inside half of a hollowed out pineapple. Another idea is to hollow out a large whole wheat bun or crusty kaiser roll. Bake the roll in a preheated 350 degree oven for about 10 minutes or until the inside of the roll is nice and crispy, and use this as a case for the salad. The leftover bread can be saved and used to make breadcrumbs.

Serves 4

1/4 cup plus 2 tablespoons nonfat yogurt
3 tablespoons light mayonnaise
salt & pepper
1/2 teaspoon curry powder
1 teaspoon Worcestershire sauce
2 cups shredded cooked chicken
1 small red apple, diced into small pieces and lightly sprinkled with lemon juice
2/3 cup diced celery
1/2 cup canned, sliced water chestnuts, drained & chopped
7 1/2 ounce can unsweetened pineapple, drained
3 tablespoons slivered, toasted almonds (optional)

Method

In a large bowl, combine yogurt, mayonnaise, salt, pepper, curry powder, and Worcestershire sauce. Add the chicken, celery, water chestnuts, apple, and pineapple, and toss to mix well. Cover and let macerate for about 20 minutes in the refrigerator. Sprinkle with slivered, toasted almonds, if desired.

Nutrient Values:

Calories:	203	Cholesterol:	56.9 mg
Protein:	21.9 g	Fiber:	1.94 g
Carbohydrates:	16.9 g	% Fat Calories:	24
Total Fat:	5.37 g		

Chicken with Dijon Mustard

This quick and easy dish is also very good cold with a tossed salad. Consider making twice as much as you need, and having it cold the next day.

Serves 6

1 tablespoon safflower oil
1 1/2 pounds boneless breast of chicken seasoned with salt (optional) and freshly ground black pepper
4 tablespoons Dijon-style mustard
4 tablespoons nonfat yogurt
2 tablespoons lite mayonnaise
1/2 cup plain dry breadcrumbs mixed together with 2 tablespoons chopped fresh basil, or 2 teaspoons dried

Method

Preheat oven to 350 degrees. Measure the oil into the baking dish, and place dish in the oven.

In a small bowl mix together mustard, yogurt, and mayonnaise. Spread each piece of chicken evenly with this mixture, then roll in breadcrumb mixture.

Place the chicken in heated baking dish, and bake for 30-35 minutes, turning once, until chicken tests done, and juices run clear when meat is pierced.

Nutrient Values:

Calories:	201	Cholesterol:	67.3 mg
Protein:	28.3 g	Fiber:	0.378 g
Carbohydrates:	8.14 g	% Fat Calories:	26
Total Fat:	5.57 g		

Chinese Stir-Fried Chicken

This super-fast, tasty meal, has endless variations and is delicious served with brown rice. When you have time, make this dish with assorted, <u>fresh</u> Chinese vegetables, (which can be prepared in advance), it is well worth the effort!

4 servings

2 tablespoons safflower oil
1 1/2 pounds skinless, boneless breast of chicken
1 package frozen chinese vegetables, thawed
3 tablespoons ginger flavor soy sauce
    <u>or</u> 3 tablespoons low sodium soy sauce
1 tablespoon fresh ginger (optional)
salt and pepper to taste

Method

In a non-stick or saute pan, heat oil until very hot. Add the chicken and stir-fry until no longer pink, only about 1 minute. Season with salt and pepper. Add soy sauce and fresh ginger and toss for a few seconds. Add the thawed chinese vegetables and cook until vegetables are warmed through. Serve with rice.

VARIATIONS: Use any combination of the following to add variety to this basic recipe.

1. Saute 1 large onion in the oil before adding the chicken breasts.
2. Marinate the pieces in the soy sauce, fresh ginger and black pepper before cooking.
3. Cook brown rice ahead of time and add to the chicken and vegetable mixture.
4. Add 2 cups of fresh bean sprouts and/or 2 cups fresh mushrooms when you add the vegetables.
5. Mix 2 cups of chicken stock with 2 tablespoons cornstarch in a small saucepan and heat until thick. Pour over the cooked chicken mixture.

This dish reheats very well and leftovers can be used up by adding extra vegetables, cooked rice, and more soy sauce and seasonings.

Nutrient Values:

Calories:	189	Cholesterol:	65.3 mg
Protein:	28.9 g	Fiber:	2.49 g
Carbohydrates:	4.73 g	% Fat Calories:	29
Total Fat:	6.21 g		

Chicken with Tomatoes and Mushrooms

This is a great luncheon dish for family or guests. The chicken can be prepared ahead of time for baking, and then refrigerated. The sauce can be made in advance also.

Serves 4

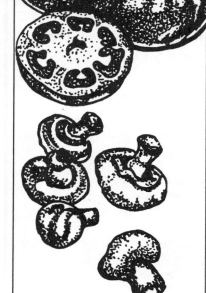

1 tablespoon safflower oil
2 whole chicken breasts, skinned, boned, and halved lengthwise
1 cup fine, dry, whole wheat bread crumbs
salt and pepper to taste
1 tablespoon fresh marjoram, (or 1 teaspoon dried)
pinch thyme
1/2 cup 1% milk
1 tablespoon safflower oil
1 tablespoon diet margarine, 40% fat
1/2 cup green onions, sliced
2 cups fresh mushrooms, sliced
8 canned plum peeled tomatoes with 1/2 cup of their juice
1/2 cup dry white wine, or 1/2 cup defatted chicken stock
1 teaspoon lemon juice
1 teaspoon fresh marjoram, or 1/8 teaspoon dried
1/8 teaspoon dried thyme

Method

Preheat oven to 350 degrees. Place baking dish in preheated oven with the oil.

Flatted chicken breasts. Mix together breadcrumbs, salt and pepper, pinch thyme, and 1 tablespoon fresh marjoram or 1 teaspoon dried. Dip chicken in milk, and then in breadcrumb mixture. Place in the baking dish that is in the oven, and bake uncovered for 15 minutes turning once very carefully in order not to disturb the crumb mixture too much.

Meanwhile make the sauce: in a non-stick skillet or saute pan heat the oil and margarine, add the green onions and saute for 1 minute. Combine the mushrooms and continue to stir and saute the mixture for 1 minute more. The mixture will be a little dry but don't worry! add the tomatoes and their juice, lemon juice, wine, and seasonings, and continue to cook until mushrooms are tender. Pour the sauce over the partly cooked chicken, spooning it over the meat to cover evenly. Bake uncovered for 5 minutes longer, or until chicken is done. This is very good served with brown rice.

Nutrient Values:

Calories:	235	Cholesterol:	68.1 mg
Protein:	29.2 g	Fiber:	0.712 g
Carbohydrates:	18.4 g	% Fat Calories:	21
Total Fat:	5.47 g		

Chicken with Currants and Apricots

A quickly prepared dish for friends or family — especially those who enjoy something sweet.

Serves 4

4 whole chicken breasts, skinned, with bone in
salt & pepper to taste
1/2 teaspoon ground ginger
1/2 cup low calorie marmalade
6 tablespoons apple juice
6 tablespoons orange juice
4 ounces dried apricots
4 ounces dried currants
1 - 2 tablespoons brown sugar

Method

Preheat oven to 350 degrees. Sprinkle the chicken with salt, pepper and ginger, coating evenly. Place in a 9 x 13 x 2 inch baking dish, and spread with the marmalade. Pour the juices into the pan. Bake, covered, for 20 minutes.

Remove from oven. Add the apricots and currants to the pan and mix well with the juices. Sprinkle the sugar over the juices. Bake, uncovered, basting the chicken frequently, until golden brown, about 15 minutes longer, or until chicken tests done. Pour the juices over the chicken and serve.

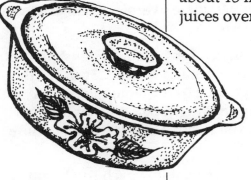

Nutrient Values:

Calories:	383	Cholesterol:	68.0 mg
Protein:	29.9 g	Fiber:	3.12 g
Carbohydrates:	66.7 g	% Fat Calories:	4
Total Fat:	1.65 g		

Cashew Chicken

This is a dish that is perfect for entertaining, since so much of it can be prepared ahead. When they are in season try using chestnuts instead of cashews - they are much lower in fat.

Serves 6

1/4 cup teriyaki sauce
2 tablespoons chopped, fresh ginger
1 1/2 pounds skinless, boneless chicken breast, cut into cubes
1 head broccoli, separated into flowerets, and stems peeled and
    sliced into medium thick slices
freshly ground black pepper
2 tablespoons safflower oil
1 teaspoon garlic powder
2 tablespoons lemon juice
1 teaspoon Worcestershire sauce
1 bunch scallions sliced. Include some of the green part also
1/2 pound sliced fresh mushrooms
1/4 cup oyster sauce
 1/4 pound snow peas
1/4 pound roasted chestnuts cut into small pieces, or raw,
    unsalted cashews

Method

Mix together the teriyaki sauce, fresh ginger and freshly ground black pepper, and place in a bowl. Add the chicken pieces and toss well to coat thoroughly. Marinate overnight if possible Drain the chicken, and save the marinade.

In a wok or large non-stick skillet, heat 2 tablespoons oil until hot. Stir fry the chicken until white and cooked. Sprinkle the chicken with garlic powder, a little of the lemon juice and Worcestershire sauce during cooking. Cook quickly in small batches so the chicken does not steam. Set aside in a medium bowl.

Stir fry onions and mushrooms, sprinkling each batch with a little lemon juice. If necessary, add 2-3 tablespoons of water or white wine if the pan seems too dry. Place the onions and mushrooms in the bowl with the chicken. Add the oyster sauce and the teriyaki marinade and mix well.

Stir-fry the broccoli in the pan with a little water, deglazing the pan as you do so. When the pan is deglazed, cover with a lid and steam for 1 minute. Add the broccoli to the chicken.

Thaw snow peas if frozen and do not cook. If fresh, cook the same as the broccoli being very careful not to overcook. Add to the other ingredients. Add the roasted chestnuts or cashews, and return all of the ingredients to the wok or skillet. Heat briefly, stirring constantly. Adjust seasonings, and serve over hot brown rice.

Nutrient Values: (using roasted chestnuts)

Calories:	295	Cholesterol:	65.3 mg
Protein:	33.8 g	Fiber:	8.47 g
Carbohydrates:	25.9 g	% Fat Calories:	21
Total Fat:	7.18 g		

Nutrient Values: (using cashews)

Calories:	358	Cholesterol:	65.3 mg
Protein:	36.1 g	Fiber:	7.14 g
Carbohydrates:	22.1 g	% Fat Calories:	38
Total Fat:	15.5 g		

Chicken Fajitas

Serve these fajitas with spicy beans, salsa, nonfat yogurt, and a salad of shredded lettuce, and chopped tomatoes

Serves 4

1/2 pound boneless breast of chicken, cut into thin strips
4 tablespoons fresh lime juice
2 teaspoons finely minced garlic cloves
1/2 teaspoon ground cumin
1 1/2 cups thinly sliced red onion
1 1/2 cups red pepper, halved, seeded, and cut into strips
1 cut sweet green pepper, halved, seeded, and cut into strips
4 flour tortillas, 10 1/2 inches in diameter
4 medium sized tomatoes, cut into chunks

Method

Combine the chicken, lime juice, garlic, and cumin in a large bowl. Marinate for at least 1 hour.

Preheat the oven to 300 degrees.

Spray a large non-stick skillet with cooking spray, and place over medium heat. Saute the onion and both peppers, for about 5 minutes, or until wilted.

Place the tortillas in the oven to warm while finishing the filling.

Add the chicken, marinade, and the tomatoes to the skillet, and cook, stirring constantly for about 3 minutes, or until cooked. Serve on warm plates with the warm tortillas on the side. Accompany with the salsa, beans, nonfat yogurt, and salad as suggested above.

Nutrient Values:

Calories:	287	Cholesterol:	32.7 mg
Protein:	19.4 g	Fiber:	4.98 g
Carbohydrates:	43.9 g	% Fat Calories:	17
Total Fat:	5.68 g		

Chicken Chili

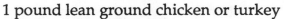

Using ground chicken or turkey instead of beef saves a lot of calories, and reduces the fat considerably. This chili tastes even better the following day — or make it early in the day for the evening meal.

Serves 6

1 pound lean ground chicken or turkey
1 large onion, chopped
1-1 pound can tomatoes, including juice
1-8 ounce can tomato puree
1 cup chicken broth
2 cups cooked or canned kidney beans
2 teaspoons chili powder
2 teaspoons finely minced garlic
1 teaspoon oregano
1 teaspoon ground cumin
1/4 teaspoon salt
1/4 teaspoon freshly ground black pepper

Method

In a non-stick, 3 quart saucepan that has been lightly sprayed with cooking spray, cook the meat until it is no longer pink, breaking it up well as you cook it. Add all the remaining ingredients. Bring to boiling, cover, and reduce the heat until the chili is slowly simmering. Cook for 1 hour. Serve with potatoes, and a large salad.

Nutrient Values:

Calories:	214	Cholesterol:	43.7 mg
Protein:	25.4 g	Fiber:	7.68 g
Carbohydrates:	24.7 g	% Fat Calories:	8
Total Fat:	2.04 g		

Chicken Salad with Honey Mustard Dressing

This delicious honey mustard dressing can be used on a plain tossed salad as well. It also makes a great dip for crudites.

Serves 6

1 1/2 pounds chicken breasts, boned, skinned and cut in half
1 1/2 cups apple juice
1 bunch scallions thinly sliced, some of the green included
2 small red apples, unpeeled, cut into medium size chunks
    sprinkled with 1 teaspoon lemon juice
1/2 cup celery cut into medium slices
1 cup seedless grapes
1/2 cup wild rice, cooked in the leftover chicken-apple broth

Dressing
1/2 cup plus 2 tablespoons plain nonfat yogurt
2 tablespoons reduced-calorie mayonnaise
2 tablespoons honey
salt & pepper to taste
2 teaspoons Dijon style mustard
lettuce leaves

Method

Prepare the dressing by mixing together all the ingredients in a small bowl. Refrigerate, covered until ready to use.

Simmer the chicken in the apple juice, using a covered saucepan over medium heat. Do not let the chicken cook in liquid that is furiously boiling! Cook until juices run clear when tested with a fork, about 15 minutes. Remove chicken from the pan and set aside to cool.

Cook the rice according to label instructions. Cut chicken into bite size cubes and mix together with the apples, grapes, celery, rice, salt and pepper. Refrigerate, covered, for at least 20 minutes so that the flavors can macerate. Add the dressing and mix well to coat evenly. Serve the salad on a bed of lettuce.

Nutrient Values:

Calories:	309	Cholesterol:	89.7 mg
Protein:	35.0 g	Fiber:	2.47 g
Carbohydrates:	25.7 g	% Fat Calories:	21
Total Fat:	7.2 g		

Chicken with Lemon and Lime

This chicken is very good cold and would be good to take along on a Summer picnic.

Serves 4

1 large lemon
1 medium lime
3 tablespoons Dijon style mustard
2 whole boneless breasts of chicken, skinned, and cut in half
1 tablespoon safflower oil
1/2 cup plain dry breadcrumbs
1/2 teaspoon salt
1/4 teaspoon white pepper
1/2 teaspoon curry powder
1 tablespoon chopped fresh oregano, (or 1 teaspoon dried)
Slices of lemon and lime for garnish

Method

Preheat oven to 350 degrees. Place 1 tablespoon oil in a 9 x 13 x 2 inch baking dish and place in the oven.

Grate 1 tablespoon rind from the lemon and 1 tablespoon rind from the lime. Squeeze 2 tablespoons juice from both the lemon and the lime. In a small bowl combine juices, zest (the rinds), and mustard. Dip the chicken into the mixture, spreading it evenly to coat well. Set aside. Mix together the breadcrumbs, salt, pepper, curry powder and oregano on a piece of wax paper. Roll the chicken in the crumb mixture, coating well on both sides, and pressing the mixture into the chicken.

Place the chicken in the baking dish in the oven, and bake for 15 minutes, uncovered. Turn chicken over and bake about 10 minutes longer or until juices run clear when pricked with a fork.

Arrange on a platter and decorate with slices of lemon and lime.

Nutrient Values:

Calories:	158	Cholesterol:	34.6 mg
Protein:	15.9 g	Fiber:	0.771 g
Carbohydrates:	11.6 g	% Fat Calories:	30
Total Fat:	5.35 g		

Chicken Cordon Bleu with White Wine Sauce

Although this excellent, classic recipe is usually made with veal, I prefer to use chicken breasts that have been pounded thin. The recipe can be made ahead up to the point indicated by asterisk.

Serves 4

2 whole chicken breasts split in half lengthwise, boned and pounded thin
freshly ground black pepper
2 tablespoons chopped fresh parsley
4 thin slices, about 2 ounces, part-skim mozzarella cheese
4 thin slices, low sodium boiled ham, about 2 ounces
1 tablespoon lite mayonnaise
1 tablespoon lemon juice
1/4 cup seasoned bread crumbs

<u>White Wine Sauce</u>

1 cup low sodium chicken stock
1/4 cup dry white wine
1/4 cup instant-blend flour
3/4 cup 2% milk
1/4 teaspoon onion powder
salt and white pepper to taste
pinch nutmeg
1 1/2 tablespoons minced fresh parsley

Method

Preheat oven to 350 degrees.

Lay the chicken cutlets out flat. Sprinkle with freshly ground black pepper, and parsley. Top each breast with a slice of cheese and half a slice of ham. Roll up tightly. Stir together mayonnaise and lemon juice in a shallow dish. Roll each cutlet in this mixture, and then in the seasoned breadcrumbs. Lightly spray a baking dish with cooking spray, and arrange the chicken pieces, seam-side down, in a single layer.* Bake in the preheated oven for 15-20 minutes, or until browned, cooked through, and the cheese is melted.

While the chicken is cooking make the sauce as follows; combine chicken broth and wine in a non-stick or heavy saucepan. Heat to boiling; then reduce heat. Mix together flour and milk in a small bowl until smooth; stir into the simmering broth. Add onion powder, nutmeg, salt and pepper and stir to mix well. Pour over the cooked chicken rolls, and sprinkle with fresh parsley.

Nutrient Values:

Calories:	235	Cholesterol:	53.9 mg
Protein:	24.5 g	Fiber:	0.562 g
Carbohydrates:	14.6 g	% Fat Calories:	24
Total Fat:	6.16 g		

Chicken A L'Orange

This fast and easy dish can be made in large quantities in a minimum amount of time. Serve this with brown rice (pouring the extra glaze over the rice if you like), and a green vegetable.

Serves 4

1 pound boneless, skinned chicken breasts, unsalted
2 cups fresh orange juice
4 teaspoons lite soy sauce
1/2 teaspoon powdered ginger
orange slices for garnish

Method

Preheat oven to 375 degrees. Rinse chicken and pat dry with paper towels. Mix together orange juice, soy sauce and ginger. Place in a small saucepan. Bring to a boil, and then lower the heat and simmer for 5 minutes or until thickened. Watch carefully so that the mixture does not evaporate too much.

Brush the chicken with the glaze, and place in an ovenproof dish. Bake, uncovered for 25 minutes, basting occasionally.

Display on a platter decorated with fresh orange slices.

Nutrient Values:

Calories:	183	Cholesterol:	65.3 mg
Protein:	27.3 g	Fiber:	0.509 g
Carbohydrates:	13.6 g	% Fat Calories:	8
Total Fat:	1.67 g		

Your Notes:

212

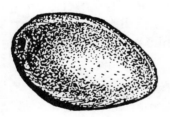

Mangoes

History: Mangoes are native to Asia and have a marvelously delicate flavor.

Nutrition: Mangoes are a good source of carotene, a compound that converts to vitamin A in the body. They are expensive, so when they are in season make the most of them!

Selection: Choose mangoes which are orange-yellow to red in color, and which give slightly with pressure. Green mangoes are hard, but can be ripened in the dark like tomatoes. Put them in a brown paper bag until they turn orange to red in color and smell fruity.

Barbecued Chicken with Mangoes and Mustard Relish

This dish is excellent when served cold. I have also found that baking the chicken instead of barbecuing it is equally as good.

Serves 4

2 teaspoons vegetable oil
1 clove garlic minced
1 teaspoon chopped green onions
1 teaspoon fresh thyme, (or 1/2 teaspoon dried thyme)
4 whole chicken breasts, skinned, with bone
1/2 cup finely chopped zucchini
1/2 cup finely chopped summer squash
1/2 cup finely chopped red onion
2 tablespoons Dijon-style mustard
2 tablespoons plain nonfat yogurt
2 medium mangoes, peeled, seeded, and sliced
lettuce leaves

Method

<u>If barbecuing:</u> Combine oil, garlic, onions and thyme, rub on chicken pieces. Grill chicken on uncovered grill, over medium heat, for 15-20 minutes. Turn, and grill chicken on the other side for 10-20 minutes more or until tender.

<u>If baking:</u> Bake the chicken in a covered baking dish in a preheated oven for 15 minutes. Remove cover, and finish cooking, uncovered, for 10-15 minutes longer or until juices run clear when tested with the point of a knife.

Meanwhile make the relish by combining zucchini, summer squash, red onion, mustard, and yogurt.

To serve, place one or two lettuce leaves on each plate and spoon on some of the relish. Next, arrange 3 mango slices on each plate, and place the cooked chicken below the slices.

Nutrient Values:

Calories:	240	Cholesterol:	68.1 mg
Protein:	29.2 g	Fiber:	4.49 g
Carbohydrates:	21.6 g	% Fat Calories:	17
Total Fat:	4.49 g		

Chicken Oregano

Use fresh oregano if you can when preparing this meal, it gives the dish a wonderful flavor.

Serves 6

2 teaspoons safflower oil
1 large onion, thinly sliced
2 garlic cloves, minced
1 1/2 cups tomato juice
2 tablespoons tomato paste
2 chicken bouillon cubes
salt and freshly ground black pepper
2 tablespoons fresh oregano, or 2 teaspoons dried
8 ounces mushrooms, sliced
1 cup 2% milk
3 pounds boneless chicken breasts, skinned and cut into 1-inch cubes

Method

Preheat the oven to 350 degrees.

Heat the oil in a non-stick casserole, and saute onion for three minutes. Add the garlic and saute for 1 minute more. Add the tomato juice, tomato paste, bouillon cubes, salt, freshly ground black pepper, oregano, mushrooms and skim milk. Stirring constantly, bring the mixture to boil. Take off the heat and add the chicken. Mix the chicken into the sauce coating well.

Cover the dish and place in the preheated 350 degree oven. Bake for 20 minutes, uncover, and cook until chicken tests done. Serve with brown rice.

Nutrient Values:

Calories:	181	Cholesterol:	66.8 mg
Protein:	28.9 g	Fiber:	1.59 g
Carbohydrates:	8.44 g	% Fat Calories:	17
Total Fat:	3.37 g		

Chicken with Plums

This dish is fast and easy to make. It looks very colorful if you serve it with two vegetables such as green beans and carrots Be sure the plums you use are sweet, or the dish will not taste good.

Serve 4

8 medium sized pitted plums, fresh or canned in lite syrup
4 tablespoons plum wine (optional)
4 whole chicken breasts, skinned, not boned

Method

Pre-heat broiler.

Puree plums and plum wine in a blender or food processor; place in a small saucepan over medium heat and bring to a boil. Reduce the heat and simmer for 8 minutes.

Brush some of the sauce over the chicken to coat lightly, and place in an ovenproof baking dish. Broil for 5 minutes. Remove from broiler, sprinkle with salt and pepper and the remaining sauce. Bake, covered, in a preheated 350 degree oven for 20 minutes; uncover and bake for 10 minutes more.

Nutrient Values:

Calories:	194	Cholesterol:	68.0 mg
Protein:	27.5 g	Fiber:	1.12 g
Carbohydrates:	17.1 g	% Fat Calories:	7
Total Fat:	1.53 g		

Turkey Meatloaf

The ingredients in this recipe can be changed according to whatever ingredients you have on hand at the time. Try your favorite meatloaf recipe substituting ground turkey for half of the ground beef.

Serves 6

2 teaspoons safflower oil
1 cup chopped onions
1 cup chopped tomatoes
1 1/2 pound ground turkey meat
1 cup seasoned breadcrumbs
1 packet low-sodium chicken stock
2 tablespoons Dijon mustard
2 egg whites
2 teaspoons spicy Dash seasoning
2 tablespoons ketchup
extra breadcrumbs

Method

Heat the oil in a nonstick pan, and saute the onions for 5 minutes. Add the tomatoes and continue for 5 minutes longer. Mix together all ingredients thoroughly, except ketchup and extra breadcrumbs. Shape into a loaf. Spread ketchup over the top of the loaf, and sprinkle breadcrumbs over ketchup.

Bake in preheated 350 degree oven for about 45 minutes. Do not overcook or the turkey loaf will be dry.

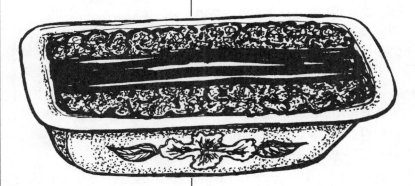

Nutrient Values:

Calories:	231	Cholesterol:	66.3 mg
Protein:	30.3 g	Fiber:	1.63 g
Carbohydrates:	17.2 g	% Fat Calories:	16
Total Fat:	4.05 g		

Creamy Turkey in French Rolls

Hollowed out whole wheat rolls make the containers for this delicious turkey filling. Serve with cranberry sauce for a sweet-sour flavor contrast.

Serves 4

4 good quality whole wheat rolls, about 4 inches in diameter
2 tablespoons butter or margarine
1 teaspoon lemon juice
1/8 teaspoon paprika
1 small clove garlic, minced
3 green onions, thinly sliced
3 tablespoons all-purpose flour
salt and pepper to taste
1 1/2 cups skim milk
1 teaspoon Dijon mustard
4 tablespoons white wine
2 cups diced cooked turkey
2 teaspoons grated lemon rind
1 tablespoon fresh basil (or 1 teaspoon dried basil)

Method

Cut the tops off the rolls, and scoop out to make a 1/2 inch thick case; set aside on a lined baking sheet. Melt 1 teaspoon butter or margarine, and add the lemon juice, paprika, and garlic. Brush the bottom of the rolls with this mixture, and bake in a 325 degree oven for about 20 minutes or until crisp inside.

In a medium sized non-stick saucepan that has been lightly sprayed with cooking spray, melt the remaining butter over medium heat. Add the green onions, and cook until limp. Stir in the flour, and a little salt and pepper; cook, stirring, until bubbly.

Remove flour mixture from heat and gradually blend in milk, and mustard. Return to heat, and cook, whisking with a small whisk, until thickened. Add the wine and stir well to mix. Mix in the turkey, and stir constantly just to heat through.

Spoon the turkey into, and over the warmed rolls. Serve immediately.

Nutrient Values:

Calories:	346	Cholesterol:	65.5 mg
Protein:	28.7 g	Fiber:	1.60 g
Carbohydrates:	28.9 g	% Fat Calories:	25
Total Fat:	9.76 g		

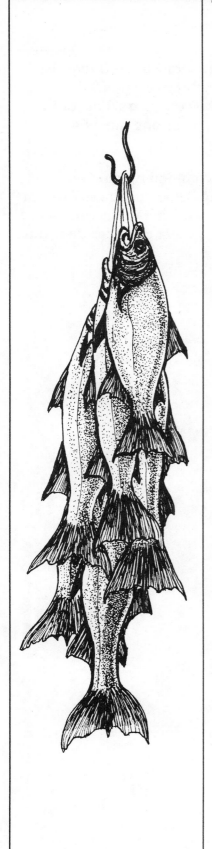

Fish Facts

Nutrition: Recent studies have shown that people who consume a diet high in fish and seafood have a lower incidence of heart disease. Credit for this effect has been given to omega-3 fatty acids, a type of polyunsaturated fat found only in marine plants and seafood. Omega-3 fatty acids are highest in fatty fishes such as salmon, bluefish, mackerel and trout, but even these fish are almost as lean as the lowest-fat red meat. Some examples of low-fat fish are perch, pike, red snapper, sea bass, sole, catfish, cod, flounder, haddock, orange roughy, and halibut.

Fish is low in sodium, with a range of 60 to 100 milligrams per 3 1/2 ounces of raw fish. Fish is also rich in potassium, iron, and phosphorous, and is low in calories. Four ounces of cod for example is only 100 calories, and 4 ounces of salmon is 240 calories. Fish is also high in protein, and 4 ounces supplies about half of the daily recommended amount.

Selecting Fish: Appearance, odor, and texture are the three important considerations when buying fish. Prepared fillets and steaks should be moist and translucent. Avoid fillets that are brown near the edges. The flesh should be elastic and spring back rapidly when pressed with a finger. Fish should always smell fresh with no "fishy" odor. Whole fish should have clear, bright eyes, firm flesh, red gills, and glistening skin.

Storing: As soon as you get the fish home, rinse it under cold water and store in airtight bags. Place the wrapped fish on top of a bowl filled with ice. Refrigerate until ready to use, preferably the day it is bought. Oily fish spoil more rapidly than lean fish. Marinate the fish for a day or two if you cannot cook them the same day.

Frozen fish: Defrost overnight in the refrigerator, or place the fish in its original wrapper in cold water. Be sure to change the water frequently until the fish thaws.

Catfish

Catfish have feelers that look like a cat's whiskers and they are found in freshwater streams and rivers throughout North America. There are several varieties; they are sold whole or in fillets and their skin which is slippery and strong must be removed before cooking.

Truly a gastronomic delight, the most common method of preparing catfish is usually deep-frying. However, these fish can be prepared by every cooking method. Low in fat, the catfish has a comparatively simple skeletal structure that provides delicious boneless eating.

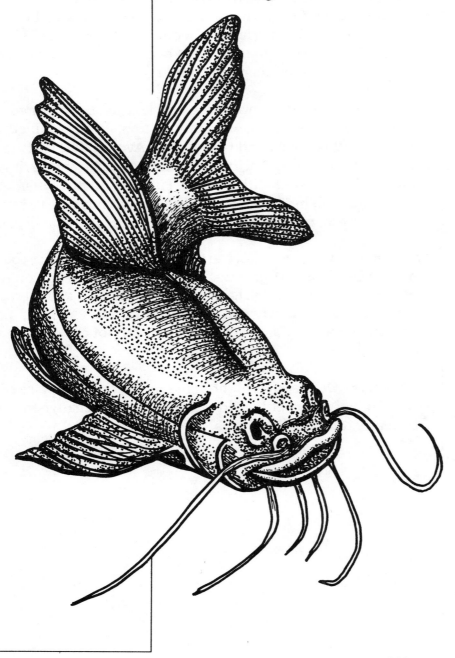

Baked Catfish with Fresh Vegetables

Use any firm fish for this delicious, quick, and easy recipe. A food processor makes the preparation of these fresh vegetables very easy.

Serves 4

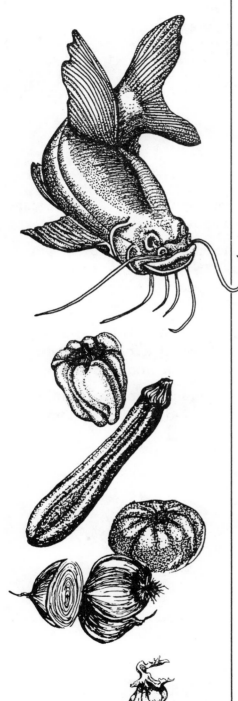

cooking spray
2 tablespoons lemon juice mixed with 1 tablespoon water
3 tablespoons chicken stock
1 medium onion thinly sliced
1 teaspoon garlic, minced
1 green pepper, seeded and diced
1 red pepper, seeded and diced
1 medium zucchini, diced
1 large tomato cut into wedges
1 tablespoon fresh oregano, or 1 teaspoon dried
1 tablespoon fresh basil, or 1 teaspoon dried
salt and freshly ground black pepper
1 1/2 pounds catfish
2 tablespoons Parmesan cheese mixed together with 3
    tablespoons seasoned breadcrumbs

Method

Preheat oven to 375 degrees. Lightly spray a large glass baking dish with cooking spray, set aside.

Sprinkle fish with lemon juice and water mixture and season with freshly ground pepper. Place in prepared baking dish.

Spray a nonstick skillet with cooking spray, and add the chicken stock. Cook the onions for 3-4 minutes. Add garlic and cook for 30 seconds. Add red and green peppers, and zucchini, and continue to cook about 4 minutes until vegetables are soft, stirring occasionally. Stir in tomato, oregano and basil. Season with salt and pepper. Spoon vegetables over the fish and sprinkle with the cheese.

Bake for about 15 minutes, or until fish is opaque. Serve with potatoes or rice.

Nutrient Values

Calories:	292	Cholesterol:	35.5 g
Protein:	35.5 g	Fiber:	3.89 g
Carbohydrates:	17.4 g	% Fat Calories:	28
Total Fat:	9.10 g		

Thawing Fish:
Thaw fish in milk to draw out the frozen taste, and provide a fresh-caught flavor.

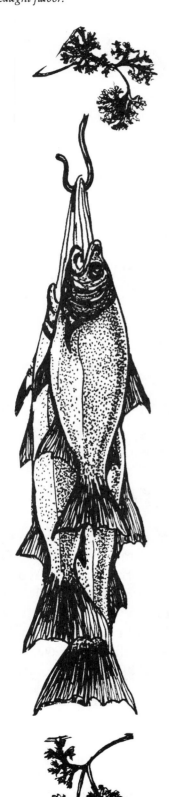

Lemon "Fried" Fish Fillets

Full of flavor, low in fat, and easy to prepare, this dish is great with a large tossed salad, or, for heartier appetites, potatoes and a vegetable.

Serves 4

1 pound flounder or other fish fillets
1/4 cup plus 1 tablespoon fine dry breadcrumbs
1 teaspoon lemon pepper seasoning
1 teaspoon parsley flakes
2 tablespoons low calorie mayonnaise
1 fresh lemon cut into wedges

Method

Preheat oven to 450 degrees.

Cut the fish into serving size pieces. Lightly spray a glass baking dish with cooking spray and set aside.

In a shallow dish, mix together the breadcrumbs, lemon pepper seasoning, and parsley flakes. Coat the fish fillets on both sides with the mayonnaise, and then press the fillets into crumb mixture to coat both sides evenly.

Bake the fish in the preheated oven for about 10-15 minutes or until the fish flakes easily when tested with a fork. Be careful not to overcook. Serve immediately with the lemon wedges.

VARIATION: Add 1 teaspoon Dijon mustard to the mayonnaise before coating the fish with it, and instead of using the lemon pepper seasoning, use 1 teaspoon paprika.

Nutrient Values:

Calories:	149	Cholesterol:	56.7 mg
Protein:	22.3 g	Fiber:	0.567 g
Carbohydrates:	6.94 g	% Fat Calories:	20
Total Fat:	3.21 g		

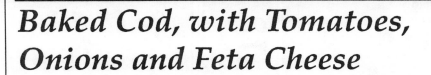

Baked Cod, with Tomatoes, Onions and Feta Cheese

This fast and easy dish can also be made with haddock or halibut.

Serves 4

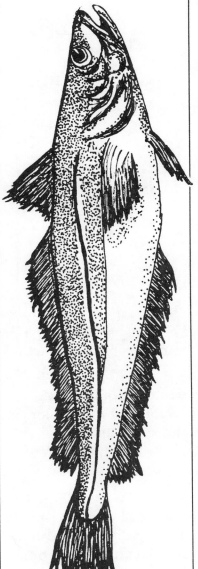

1 pound cod steaks
2 teaspoons safflower oil
1 large onion sliced
2 teaspoons fresh garlic, minced
2 large, fresh tomatoes, or 4 canned tomatoes
2 tablespoons chopped fresh oregano, (or 2 teaspoons dried)
1/4 cup dry white wine, or 1/4 cup clam juice
1/3 cup crumbled feta cheese
3 tablespoons chopped fresh parsley
freshly ground black pepper

Method

Preheat oven to 375 degrees. Lightly spray a large glass baking dish with cooking spray and set aside.

Lightly spray a nonstick saute pan or frying pan, and saute onion and garlic in the oil until onion is soft. Add the oregano and tomatoes, and simmer for 2-3 minutes.

Layer tomatoes onions, garlic and oregano in the bottom of the dish. Divide the fish into 4 pieces and arrange on top of the vegetables. Sprinkle the wine evenly over the fish.

Cover the dish with foil and bake until it is firm to the touch about 15-20 minutes. Sprinkle the fish with feta cheese, parsley and a little black pepper. spoon the juices in the pan over the fish. Serve immediately.

Nutrient Values:

Calories:	170	Cholesterol:	55.0 mg
Protein:	22.5 g	Fiber:	1.64 g
Carbohydrates:	6.68 g	% Fat Calories:	27
Total Fat:	4.82 g		

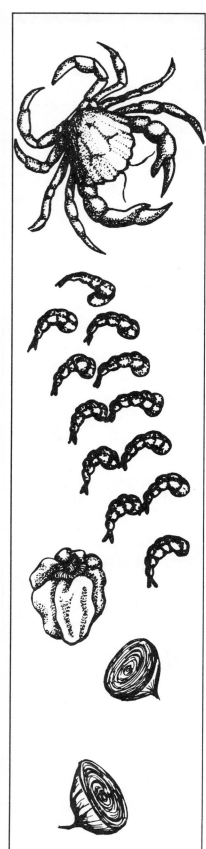

Sole Stuffed with Crabmeat and Shrimp

This is a very special dish that can be made up in large quantities for entertaining. Be very careful not to buy the sole too thin, or the filling will split the fish as it cooks. Flounder can be substituted for the sole.

Serves 6

1 pound dover sole, about 1/2 inch thick
lemon juice for sprinkling the sole
2 teaspoons safflower oil
1/2 cup finely chopped onion
1/2 teaspoon garlic
1/2 cup finely chopped green pepper
2 teaspoons lemon juice
6 ounces chopped shrimp, or 6 ounces baby shrimp
2 ounces crabmeat, shredded
Dash of hot pepper sauce
salt and pepper to taste
1 tablespoon melted butter

Method

Sprinkle the sole with a little lemon juice and set aside. Spray a baking dish with cooking spray and set aside. Preheat oven to 375 degrees.

In a nonstick saute pan heat the oil, and saute the onion for 2-3 minutes. Add the garlic and continue to saute for 1 minute longer. Add the green pepper and lemon juice, and saute until the vegetables are soft. Mix in the shrimp and crabmeat, and a few drops of hot pepper sauce. Taste, and add salt and pepper if necessary.

Divide the filling between the sole fillets, and roll up from the wider end. Place seam-side down in the baking dish and pour the melted butter over the fillets. Bake for about 20 minutes or until the fish is done. Serve with baked potato or rice, a green vegetable, and a large, mixed salad.

Nutrient Values:

Calories:	191	Cholesterol:	146 mg
Protein:	31.1 g	Fiber:	0.361 g
Carbohydrates:	2.39 g	% Fat Calories:	29
Total Fat:	5.95 g		

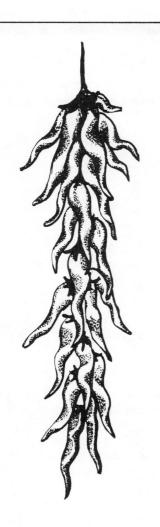

Sea Bass with Chilies and Yogurt

If you like chilies, you will enjoy this easy to prepare fish dish.

Serves 4

1 1/2 pounds sea bass, or sea trout fillets
salt and pepper to taste
2 tablespoons fresh lemon juice
1/2 cup nonfat yogurt
2 tablespoons scallions
4 teaspoons minced, fresh chilies
1 tablespoon chopped fresh chives

Method

Preheat oven to 400 degrees.

Lightly spray a baking dish with cooking spray, and arrange the fillets in a single layer in the dish. Sprinkle with salt, pepper and lemon juice.

Combine the yogurt, scallions, chilies, and chives, and stir well to mix. Taste, and season with a little salt and pepper, and more chilies if necessary. Spoon over the fillets. Bake for about 10-15 minutes, or until fish is opaque. Be careful not to overcook. Serve with a baked potato, green vegetables, and salsa.

Nutrient Values:

Calories:	207	Cholesterol:	117 mg
Protein:	33.0 g	Fiber:	0.150 g
Carbohydrates:	2.17 g	% Fat Calories:	29
Total Fat:	6.53 g		

Trout with Mushroom Sauce

This delicious, fast and easy recipe, takes only minutes to prepare and about 10 minutes to cook.

Serves 4

8 ounces mushrooms, sliced
2 teaspoons safflower oil
1 teaspoon minced garlic
6 tablespoons chicken broth
1/4 cup dry sherry
1 pound sea trout
2 tablespoons lime juice
salt and freshly ground black pepper
2 tablespoons chopped fresh parsley

Method

Preheat oven to 425 degrees. Spray a nonstick skillet with cooking spray.

Heat the oil in the skillet and saute mushrooms and garlic in the oil for about two minutes. Add the chicken broth and dry sherry. Sprinkle with a little salt and pepper. Cook for 1 minute longer.

Place the fish in a glass baking dish that has been lightly sprayed with cooking spray. Sprinkle the fish with the lime juice. Pour mushroom sauce over the fish.

Bake for about 10 minutes or until fish is opaque. Sprinkle with parsley and serve.

Nutrient Values:

Calories:	202	Cholesterol:	82.8 mg
Protein:	30.3 g	Fiber:	0.089 g
Carbohydrates:	0.760 g	% Fat Calories:	29
Total Fat:	6.49 g		

Broiled Cod Steaks with Fresh Herbs and Garlic

These meaty steaks are very filling, and delicious. Try to use fresh fish. I really feel freezing fish destroys much of its delicate flavor.

Serves 6

2 pounds cod steaks, about 1 inch thick
1 teaspoon minced garlic
2 tablespoons unsalted butter
1 onion, minced
2 tablespoons chopped fresh chives
salt and freshly ground black pepper
2 tablespoons lemon juice
1 1/2 tablespoons chopped, fresh parsley

Method

Preheat broiler

In a non-stick skillet lightly sprayed with cooking spray, melt 1 tablespoon of butter and saute the onion over medium heat until soft. Add the garlic and cook 2 minutes longer. Add salt, pepper, chives, lemon juice, and remaining butter, and heat until melted.

Place fish on the broiler pan, and brush with some of the onion mixture. Broil about 2-3 inches from the heat for 3-4 minutes, brushing with more of the onion mixture once or twice. Carefully turn the fish over, and broil 4-5 minutes longer, brushing with the remaining mixture. Fish is done when it flakes easily. Be very careful not to overcook. Serve immediately, sprinkled with the chopped parsley.

Nutrient Values:

Calories:	170	Cholesterol:	75.4 mg
Protein:	27.4 g	Fiber:	0.544 g
Carbohydrates:	2.83 g	% Fat Calories:	27
Total Fat:	4.94 g		

Baked Sole Italian Style

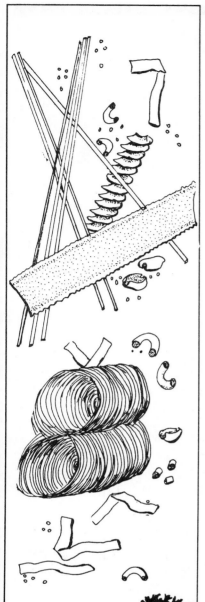

Fresh oregano can now be found in many supermarkets - and it is wonderful! However, in a pinch, you can substitute dried oregano. Do be sure that you use good tasting tomatoes. If none are available, use canned, Italian plum tomatoes, peeled. This recipe is fast, easy and delicious, and is good served with pasta.

Serves 4

2 pounds thick flounder or sole
1 yellow onion, sliced wafer thin
2 teaspoons garlic, crushed
1 tablespoon safflower oil
2 tomatoes, fresh or canned, peeled, seeded, and chopped
3 tablespoons fresh oregano or 1 tablespoon dried
salt and freshly ground black pepper
foil for cooking the fish

Method

Preheat the oven to 350 degrees. Heat the oil, and saute the onion and garlic for 3-4 minutes or until soft. Add the tomatoes, oregano, salt, and pepper, and saute for 1 minute more.

Rinse fish and pat dry. Arrange the fish fillets on the foil and cover with the tomato-oregano mixture. Wrap the fish in the foil, being careful to fold the edges of the foil over so that no juices will spill out, and place in a 13 x 9 x 2 baking dish. Bake for 15 minutes, or until fish flakes easily when tested with a fork. Be careful when you unwrap the fish as it will be steaming.

Nutrient Values:

Calories:	179	Cholesterol:	72.6 mg
Protein:	29.3 g	Fiber:	1.28 g
Carbohydrates:	4.69 g	% Fat Calories:	22
Total Fat:	4.27 g		

Saute of Bluefish with Fresh Herbs and Lime Juice

If you are lucky enough to have access to good, fresh bluefish, you will really enjoy this recipe.

Serves 4

1 pound bluefish or sea trout fillets, cut into 4 serving pieces
2 tablespoons flour seasoned with 1/4 teaspoon salt and freshly ground black pepper
2 teaspoons safflower oil
2 tablespoons clam juice or chicken stock
4 scallions, trimmed and thinly sliced
1/4 cup garlic flavored red wine vinegar
2 teaspoons honey
2 tablespoons fresh lime
4 canned plum tomatoes, peeled, or 2 large, very ripe fresh tomatoes
2 tablespoons tomato juice
1/4 cup chopped fresh basil or 1/4 cup fresh parsley

Method

Dust fillets with the seasoned flour, shaking off the excess.

In a nonstick skillet that has been sprayed with cooking spray, heat the oil over medium heat. Add the fillets and saute on one side for 4 minutes. Turn, season with a little black pepper, and cook for about three or four more minutes or until the fish is cooked and feels firm to the touch. Transfer to a platter and keep warm.

Heat the chicken stock or clam juice in the skillet, and add the remaining ingredients. Cook for 2 minutes, stirring constantly. Spread evenly over the fish. Serve immediately.

Nutrient Values:

Calories:	223	Cholesterol:	66.9 mg
Protein:	23.8 g	Fiber:	1.15 g
Carbohydrates:	15.6 g	% Fat Calories:	29
Total Fat:	7.28 g		

Red Snapper with Oregano and Anchovies

This tasty fish dish is very fast and easy to prepare. Rinsing the anchovies first, will remove the excess salt

Serves 6

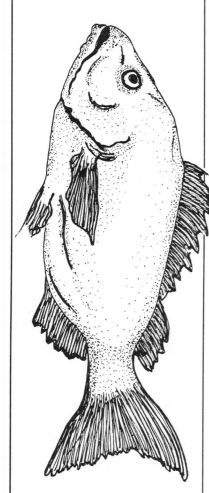

1 1/2 pounds red snapper
2 tablespoons lemon juice
salt and freshly ground black pepper
1 tablespoon safflower oil
1 can (2 ounces) anchovy fillets, drained, rinsed, and patted dry
2 tablespoons fresh oregano, or 2 teaspoons dried
1/2 cup seasoned breadcrumbs
2 tablespoons chopped parsley

Method

Preheat oven to 400 degrees. Lightly spray a glass baking dish with cooking spray.

Place the fish in the baking dish, and sprinkle with lemon juice and salt and pepper.

In a small non-stick skillet, heat the oil over medium heat. Add the anchovies and herbs. Cook for about 2 minutes, or until the anchovies are well dissolved. Add the breadcrumbs and parsley and continue to cook for 1 minute longer. Coat this mixture evenly over the fish, and bake in the preheated oven for about 8 minutes, or until the fish is opaque. This is very good served with brown rice and ratatouille.

Nutrient Values

Calories:	182	Cholesterol:	48.9 mg
Protein:	26.4 g	Fiber:	0.497 g
Carbohydrates:	6.93 g	% Fat Calories:	24
Total Fat:	4.73 g		

Red Snapper with Red Peppers, Onions and White Wine

This simple to prepare fish dish is incredibly tasty, especially when you use fresh tarragon. Set a timer so that you don't overcook the fish; it becomes very dry when overdone.

Serves 6

1 1/2 pounds red snapper fillets, fresh if possible
2 tablespoons lemon juice
1/4 cup dry white wine, or 1/4 cup clam juice
1 tablespoon safflower oil
1 large yellow onion, diced
1 large red pepper, diced
1/2 pound mushrooms, sliced
1/4 cup fresh tarragon, or 1 tablespoon plus 1 teaspoon dried
freshly ground black pepper

Method

Preheat oven to 350 degrees. In a shallow rectangular baking dish, sprinkle the snapper fillets with lemon juice, and then pour the wine or the clam juice over them.

In a large nonstick saute or frying pan, heat the oil until very hot. Add the onion and saute for about 4 minutes, and then add the red pepper. Continue to saute the ingredients in the pan for 3 minutes more, add the mushroom slices and the minced tarragon. Grind the black pepper over the mixture, and saute for 1 minute longer.

Cover the fish with the vegetables, and cover the baking dish with foil. Bake in a preheated oven for 15 minutes, or until the fish flakes easily when tested with a fork.

Nutrient Values:

Calories:	177	Cholesterol:	42.0 mg
Protein:	25.2 g	Fiber:	1.98 g
Carbohydrates:	7.75 g	% Fat Calories:	23
Total Fat:	4.34 g		

Curried Shrimp

This is a very good tasting "medium hot curry." If you prefer a milder curry, cut the curry powder down to 1 tablespoon.

Serves 6-8

1 tablespoon safflower oil
1 medium onion, chopped
1 clove garlic, minced
1 stalk celery, diced
2 tablespoons curry powder
1 tablespoon tomato paste
2 cups chicken stock
1 banana cut into thick slices
1 apple cut into cubes
2 pounds shrimp, peeled, and deveined
salt and pepper to taste

Method

In a large nonstick fry-pan or saute pan, saute the onion and garlic in 2 teaspoons oil for 2 minutes. Add the celery, and saute 1 minute more. Stir in the curry powder, tomato paste, and chicken stock and mix well. Add banana and apple, bring to a boil, reduce heat, and simmer for 10 minutes. Set aside curry mixture to cool.

Heat the remaining teaspoon of oil in a nonstick saucepan or skillet, and saute the shrimp for 2 minutes. Sprinkle with salt and pepper to taste and remove from the heat.

Puree the curry mixture in a blender or food processor until smooth. Return to pan to reheat. Add the shrimp and serve over rice.

Nutrient Values: (for 8 servings)

Calories:	188	Cholesterol:	173 mg
Protein:	25.0 g	Fiber:	1.96 g
Carbohydrates:	11.7 g	% Fat Calories:	22
Total Fat:	4.47 g		

Island Seafood Salad

This is a very attractive looking salad that always gets lots of compliments when it is served. Fresh, warm, whole wheat rolls are an excellent accompaniment.

Serves 4

2 papayas, peeled, seeded and sliced
2 mangoes, peeled, seeded and sliced
1/2 fresh pineapple cut into cubes
2 kiwi fruit, sliced
1 1/2 pounds medium shrimp, peeled, deveined and cooked
1 1/2 pounds fresh crabmeat

Dressing
1/2 cup nonfat yogurt mixed with 1-2 tablespoons honey
2 tablespoons unsweetened coconut, flaked
2 tablespoons lemon juice
1 tablespoon grated lemon rind
1 teaspoon grated fresh ginger
2 tablespoons low-calorie mayonnaise

Method

Arrange fruit attractively on lettuce on a large platter.

Combine the dressing ingredients, and mix well. Add the cooked shrimp and the crab and stir just to coat evenly.

Serve well chilled in a large bowl. or on individual plates atop lettuce.

Nutrient Values:

Calories:	316	Cholesterol:	124.0 mg
Protein:	24.9 g	Fiber:	6.06 g
Carbohydrates:	45.9 g	% Fat Calories:	16
Total Fat:	5.95 g		

Shrimp Salad with Grapes

Make this salad for a light lunch or dinner and serve it on a bed of lettuce. Decorate each plate with lemon wedges, and accompany with fresh fruit and the best whole wheat rolls you can find.

Serves 4

2 tablespoons low-calorie mayonnaise
6 tablespoons plain nonfat yogurt
1 tablespoon lemon juice
1 teaspoon grated lemon peel
1/8 teaspoon tarragon, crushed
salt and pepper
1 pound fresh shrimp, peeled and deveined
1 1/2 cups diced celery
1 cup red grapes

Method

Combine mayonnaise, yogurt, lemon juice, lemon peel, tarragon, salt and pepper. Add remaining ingredients and toss to coat well. Chill for at least 30 minutes. Serve as suggested above.

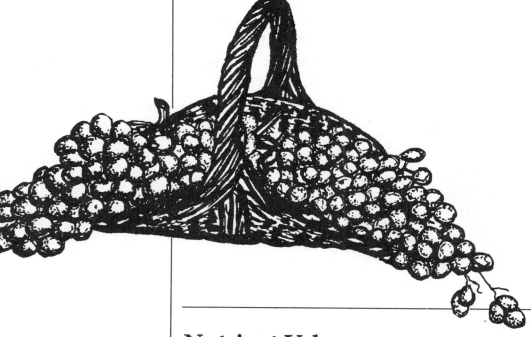

Nutrient Values:

Calories:	186	Cholesterol:	175 mg
Protein:	24.8 g	Fiber:	1.26 g
Carbohydrates:	13.0 g	% Fat Calories:	18
Total Fat:	3.74 g		

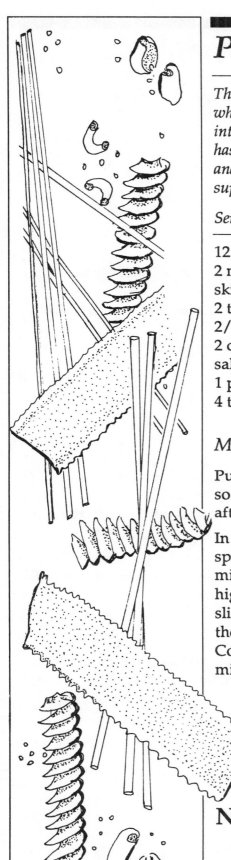

Pasta with Bay Scallops

The scallops in this recipe are in a cream sauce, which is made with whole milk instead of heavy cream. Once you begin to reduce your fat intake, whole milk begins to taste like cream anyway, and of course it has a lot less fat. It is important to peel the red peppers for this recipe, and if you use fresh pastas, (now available in many gourmet shops or supermarkets) you will quickly create a truly gourmet, low fat meal!

Serves 4

12 ounces fresh pasta or 8 ounces dried
2 medium sized red bell peppers, membrane, seeds, and outer skin removed
2 teaspoons unsalted butter
2/3 cup chopped scallions, (the white and green part)
2 cups whole milk
salt and white pepper to taste
1 pound bay scallops
4 tablespoons fresh parsley, minced

Method

Put the water on to boil for cooking the pasta, and time the pasta so it will be done when the sauce is finished, (about 5 minutes after you begin the sauce.)

In a medium nonstick skillet that has been sprayed with cooking spray, melt the butter over medium heat. Saute scallions for 1 minute. Add the milk and white pepper, and turn the heat up to high. Reduce milk for 1-2 minutes until it starts to thicken slightly, watch it carefully so it doesn't reduce too much. Reduce the heat to medium and then add the scallops and salt to taste. Cook only for 30 seconds. Add the peeled red peppers and cook 1 minute longer. Serve over the hot, well drained pasta.

Nutrient Values:

Calories:	332	Cholesterol:	59.1 mg
Protein:	28.0 g	Fiber:	2.66 g
Carbohydrates:	37.1 g	% Fat Calories:	21
Total Fat:	7.52 g		

Spicy Chinese Shrimp

This recipe is a favorite of mine, and does not take long to prepare.

Serves 4

2 teaspoons safflower oil
1 cup diced green pepper
1 cup diced red pepper
1 cup chopped leeks
1 teaspoon minced garlic
2 teaspoons fresh, minced ginger root
1 teaspoon mongolian fire oil, (found in supermarkets with the chinese foods)
1 pound large shrimp, peeled, deveined, and cut in half lengthwise
1/2 cup chicken stock
2 tablespoons dry vermouth or dry sherry
2 tablespoons ketchup
2 teaspoons cornstarch
1/2 teaspoon honey

Method

In a large non-stick skillet or wok that has been lightly sprayed with cooking spray, heat the oil until hot. Add the next five ingredients, and saute for about 2 minutes until just tender but still crisp. Remove from skillet and set aside.

Heat the mongolian fire oil and add the shrimp. Saute until just pink, being careful not to overcook. Return the vegetables to the skillet, and stir to combine well. Remove pan from heat while mixing the sauce ingredients.

In a small bowl, mix together chicken stock, sherry, ketchup, cornstarch, and honey. Mix very well to dissolve cornstarch. Return the pan to the heat and pour the sauce ingredients into the skillet, stirring constantly until mixture comes to a boil and becomes thick. Serve over rice.

Nutrient Values:

Calories:	189	Cholesterol:	172.0 mg
Protein:	24.3 g	Fiber:	0.875 g
Carbohydrates:	8.01 g	% Fat Calories:	29
Total Fat:	5.75 g		

Scallop Curry with Tarragon Brown Rice

Unlike the shrimp curry this one is very, very mild. You could even leave out the curry powder if you prefer.

Serves 4

Tarragon Brown Rice
1 cup uncooked brown rice
1 cup clam juice or chicken broth
1 1/2 cups cold water
3/4 teaspoon salt
1 teaspoon butter
3 tablespoons freshly chopped tarragon

Method

In a 3 quart saucepan with a tight fitting lid, heat the water, clam juice, salt and brown rice, until boiling. Cover and cook on low heat for 45 minutes. DO NOT REMOVE THE LID. Remove from heat. Allow rice to steam covered for 10 to 15 minutes. Add the freshly chopped tarragon, and keep warm.

Bay Scallops
1 teaspoon butter
1 teaspoon safflower oil
1 pound sea scallops
salt and pepper to taste
1 teaspoon curry powder
1/4 cup clam juice or chicken stock
1 tablespoon lemon juice
1 tablespoon chopped fresh parsley

Method

In a medium sized skillet, heat the butter and oil until hot. Add the scallops and cook until opaque, about 2 minutes. Sprinkle with curry powder, salt and pepper and mix well. Cook 1-2 minutes more. Remove scallops from the pan and keep them warm. Add clam juice, lemon juice, and parsley to the skillet. Stir, scraping brown bits from the bottom of the pan. Pour the sauce over the scallops, and serve with the tarragon brown rice.

Nutrient Values:

Calories:	312	Cholesterol:	42.9 mg
Protein:	24.5 g	Fiber:	1.90 g
Carbohydrates:	40.0 g	% Fat Calories:	16
Total Fat:	5.40 g		

Desserts, Cakes, and Cookies

When it comes to reducing the fat content in our diet, desserts, cakes, and cookies are where we can really fail miserably. This section has many delicious desserts, cakes, and cookies that are not high in fat, and yet full of flavor, including a chocolate pound cake. Enjoy these items, but as with all recipes containing sugar, eat them in moderation.

Desserts, Cakes and Cookies

Strawberry-Raspberry Souffle

You can use all strawberries or all raspberries if you like, either fresh or frozen. If using frozen be very sure the fruit is well thawed and drained, or the excess water will break down this delicate mixture.

Serves 6

2/3 cup water
2 cups frozen raspberries, thawed and well drained,
    or 2 half-pints fresh raspberries
2 cups frozen strawberries, thawed and well drained,
    or 2 half-pints fresh
2 tablespoons Grand Marnier, triple-sec, or strawberry nectar
1/2 cup fruit juice reserved from frozen berries,
    or 1/2 cup strawberry nectar
2 tablespoons fresh lemon juice
2 envelopes plain gelatin
1/2 cup plus 2 tablespoons sugar
2/3 cup instant nonfat dry milk powder
4 egg whites
additional fruit for decoration

Method

Place 2/3 cup of water in freezer for about 25 minutes or until ice begins to form over surface.

Cut a piece of aluminum foil long enough to fit around a 1 1/2 - 2 quart souffle or straight-sided dish. Allow 3-4 inches overlap. Fold lengthwise into half and wrap foil around dish to form collar. Secure foil with string or freezer tape, but secure it well. Lightly spray dish and collar with cooking spray. Set aside.

Puree the fruit in a food processor together with either the Grand Marnier, triple-sec, or strawberry nectar. Set aside.

Pour the fruit nectar or reserved juice into a small saucepan and sprinkle the gelatin over it. Let stand for 1 minute. Dissolve over low heat stirring constantly. Do not allow mixture to boil, but make sure it is hot enough to dissolve the sugar. Stir in 1/4 cup sugar, and lemon juice; mix well. Add to the fruit puree in the food processor and process for 2 seconds. Remove mixture to a large bowl, and refrigerate while preparing rest of souffle. Stir once or twice.

In a chilled bowl with chilled beaters mix together the ice cold water with the milk powder, and beat on high speed for 5 minutes or until stiff peaks form. Set aside.

Beat together the egg whites and cream of tartar until soft peaks form. Slowly begin to add the remaining sugar, 1 tablespoon at a time and continue to beat until stiff peaks form. Take 1/4 of the egg whites and stir into the fruit puree to lighten it. Fold the rest of the egg white mixture into the lightened puree mixture in 3 stages. Continue to fold adding milk powder mixture. Spoon the mixture into the prepared dish, and chill for 4 hours or longer. Decorate with fresh raspberries or strawberries.

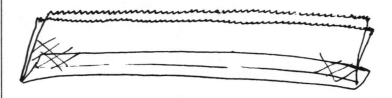

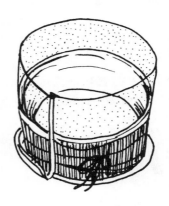

Nutrient Values:

Calories:	199	Cholesterol:	1.38 mg
Protein:	8.15 g	Fiber:	6.84 g
Carbohydrates:	42.3 g	% Fat Calories:	3
Total Fat:	0.746 g		

Banana Blackberry Mousse

This pleasant tasting dessert is also a good source of fiber.

Serves 4

1/4 cup apple juice
1 packet unflavored gelatin
2 bananas
1 cup blackberries
2 tablespoons lemon juice
grated rind of lemon
2 tablespoons blackberry brandy
1/2 cup blackberry, banana, or plain nonfat yogurt
1 egg white
artificial sweetener to **equal 2** tablespoons sugar, or 2 tablespoons
sugar (optional)

Method

Sprinkle gelatin over apple juice in a small saucepan. Let stand
for 1 minute. Stir over low heat until completely dissolved.
Remove from heat and let stand until lukewarm.

Combine all ingredients in a blender or food processor for 1
minute. Pour into individual serving dishes, or a glass dessert
dish. Serve with creamy whipped cream, or whipped cream topping.

VARIATIONS: Use strawberries with strawberry liquer, or raspberries with raspberry liquer.

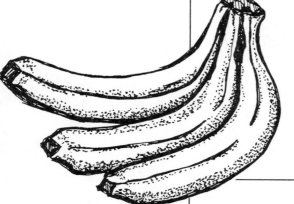

Nutrient Values:

Calories:	11 9	Cholesterol:	0.500 mg
Protein:	2.74 g	Fiber:	3.28 g
Carbohydrates:	24.4 g	% Fat Calories:	4
Total Fat:	0.536 g		

Raspberry Parfait

This delightful dessert is fast and easy to make. After pureeing the berries adjust the sweetness according to your taste. Substitute strawberries or blueberries for a change.

Serves 4

12 ounces fresh or frozen raspberries
2 tablespoons raspberry liquer (optional)
1 1/2 cups raspberry lowfat yogurt
1 - 2 tablespoons sugar or other sweetener
4 raspberries for decoration

Method

Puree the berries in a blender or food processor for a few seconds. Set aside. Taste for sweetness and add sugar or liquer if desired. Process for 2 seconds longer.

Spoon the berries and yogurt alternately into chilled parfait or wine glasses, ending with the yogurt. Top wih a raspberry and serve cold.

Nutrient Values:

Calories:	160	Cholesterol:	3.75 mg
Protein:	4.53 g	Fiber:	5.41 g
Carbohydrates:	34.7 g	% Fat Calories:	7
Total Fat:	1.39 g		

Fruit Filled Papayas with Lemon Rum Sauce

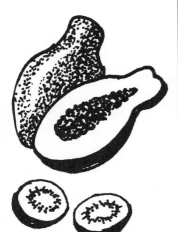

Make this in the summertime when these tropical fruits are at their best. The rum sauce is excellent over frozen yogurt, and also compliments any other fruit salad that contains strawberries and bananas. Be sure to use a 10-inch skillet when you make the sauce or it will not reduce rapidly.

Serves 6

Sauce
2-12 ounce cans banana-strawberry nectar
2 tablespoons lemon juice
4 tablespoons dark rum

<u>Fruit Salad</u>
3 very large, fresh papayas
1 kiwi fruit, peeled and sliced, the slices cut in half
1 pint strawberries, washed and sliced
1 banana, peeled and sliced
1 mango, peeled and diced

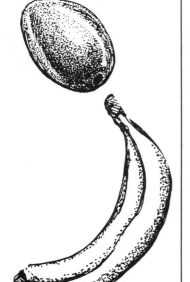

Method

Make the sauce by combining 1 1/2 cans of the strawberry-banana nectar with the lemon juice and rum in a 10-inch skillet. Boil for 5-10 minutes or until syrupy. Set aside to cool.

Cut papayas in half and scoop out seeds. Fill with remaining fruit. Cover with sauce and chill before serving.

Nutrient Values:

Calories:	220	Cholesterol:	0 mg
Protein:	2.22 g	Fiber:	7.44 g
Carbohydrates:	50.1 g	% Fat Calories:	4
Total Fat:	0.890 g		

Bananas with Pineapple-Rum Sauce

It is important to use a 10-inch skillet when you make this syrup, as using a smaller one will take much longer to reduce nectar. This is a most attractive looking, delicious dessert.

Serves 4

1-12 ounce can banana-pineapple nectar
    (found in supermarkets with the unfrozen juices)
2 tablespoons dark rum
3 bananas
lemon juice
1 1/2 cups frozen yogurt, vanilla, banana, or pineapple flavor
Mint sprig for garnishing

Method

Preheat oven to 350 degrees.

Prepare the bananas by cutting in half crosswise, and then lengthwise. You will have 12 pieces - 3 for each person. Brush the bananas with a little lemon juice. Spray a pan or baking dish with nonstick vegetable spray, and bake the bananas for 5 minutes. Do not overcook.

Meanwhile, make a syrup by combining the nectar and rum in a 10-inch skillet. Boil, uncovered for 5-10 minutes or until the sauce is reduced to 1/2 cup.

Place some of the sauce on each dessert plate. Place 3 banana pieces on top of the sauce in a fan shape. Place two tablespoons of yogurt at the base of the bananas on each plate. Garnish with a mint sprig.

Nutrient Values:

Calories:	222	Cholesterol:	3.75 mg
Protein:	4.66 g	Fiber:	1.84 g
Carbohydrates:	46.5 g	% Fat Calories:	6
Total Fat:	1.36 g		

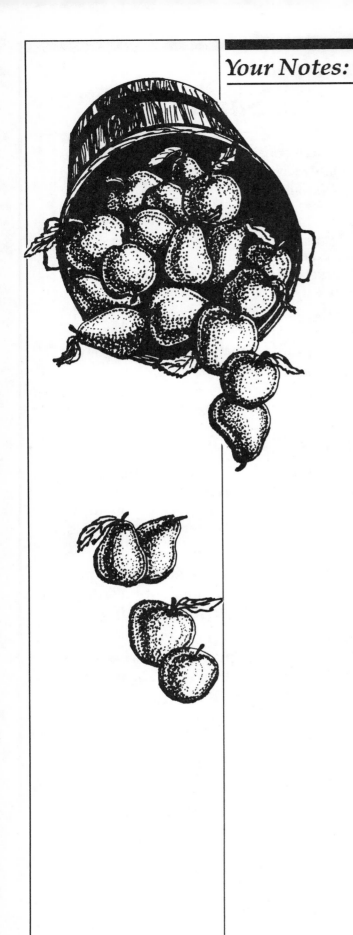

Blueberries

Nutrition: Blueberries are a good source of vitamin C to the diet. They also contribute fiber; are low in sodium (9 mg per 1 cup serving); and provide about 82 calories per cup.

Selecting: Look for plump, fresh berries when purchasing, and avoid any baskets that are leaking.

Storing: Keep fresh blueberries cold and covered, and use within 2-3 days for peak freshness. Rinse gently just before using, don't rinse ahead of time or they will go mushy.

Ways With Blueberries: Toss fresh blueberries on your breakfast cereal for an eye-opening taste.

Add blueberries to fresh fruit salads.

Fold fresh blueberries into your pancake mix and serve for breakfast or lunch. Top with nonfat yogurt mixed with a little honey or sugar.

Fold fresh blueberries into cottage cheese or yogurt.

Make fresh blueberry sauce to serve over lowfat frozen yogurt, or angel food cake.

Pack clean, dry, fresh blueberries in freezer containers for later use in baking.

Individual Blueberry Cobblers

Cobblers are one of my favorite foods. I make them for breakfast, lunch, or dessert! This can also be made in a 2-quart baking dish.

Serves 4

---

4 cups fresh or frozen blueberries
8 tablespoons sugar
2/3 cup all-purpose flour
1 teaspoon baking powder
1/4 teaspoon salt
1/8 teaspoon cinnamon
1/8 teaspoon nutmeg
4 tablespoons unsalted butter
1/2 teaspoon vanilla
8 tablespoons 2% low fat milk

Method

Pre-heat oven to 400 degrees.

Lightly spray the individual souffle dishes with cooking spray. Divide the berries between the dishes and sprinkle with two tablespoons of the sugar.

Mix together flour, baking powder, salt, cinnamon, and nutmeg, and set aside.

In a food processor or electric mixer, beat together the remaining sugar, butter, and vanilla until light and fluffy. Add the flour mixture to the creamed mixture alternately with milk, beating until smooth. Spread over the berries.

Place the dishes on a baking sheet that has been covered with foil, and bake for 35-40 minutes, until the topping is well browned and springs back when the center is touched in the middle. Allow to cool slightly before serving.

Nutrient Values:

Calories:	374	Cholesterol:	33.8 mg
Protein:	4.36 g	Fiber:	4.48 g
Carbohydrates:	63.4 g	% Fat Calories:	30
Total Fat:	12.9 g		

Apples

History: Apples have been cultivated for more than three thousand years, since they were developed from the wild crabapple. Crabapples provide a jelly with a wonderful flavor and color.

Nutrition: Apples are the fruit that many people count on for instant goodness. They are a good source of roughage, minerals and vitamin C, the amount of vitamin C depends on upon the ripeness of the apple.

Yield: 1 pound of apples will give about 3 cups of slices or 1 1/3 cups applesauce. There are about 3 medium sized apples to the pound.

Selecting: Look for apples that are green around the stem and flower ends; they have much more flavor than all red or completely golden ones. For eating, Baldwin, Delicious, Golden Delicious, Granny Smith, McIntosh, Pippin, and Winesap are good choices. For baking, Rome Beauty, Jonathan and Northern Spry are good. For great pies, use Granny Smith, Pippin, Greening and Northern Spry.

Hints: Rub the cut surface of an apple with lemon juice to keep it from turning brown.

Apple Pudding

This satisfying dessert is good to eat anytime of the year. Be sure to cool the pudding before adding the yogurt topping, or else serve it separately.

Serves 8

2 pounds apples
6 whole cloves
1/2 cup light brown sugar
grated rind of 1 lemon
2 cups dry whole-wheat bread crumbs
1 teaspoon ground cinnamon
1 cup raisins
1 whole egg
2 egg whites
1 cup nonfat yogurt mixed together with 2 tablespoons honey or other sweetener

Method

Preheat oven to 350 degrees. Lightly spray an 8-inch spring form cake pan with cooking spray.

Peel and core the apples and cook them in a medium saucepan with 1 tablespoon water, 6 whole cloves and 3 tablespoons light brown sugar. Stir in grated rind of 1 lemon, and set aside to cool.

Mix breadcrumbs together with the remaining sugar, and the cinnamon. Set aside. Remove the cloves from the apples, and add the raisins to the apple mixture.

Beat together the egg and 2 egg whites and combine with the apple and raisin mixture. Spoon one third into the prepared pan. Smooth to make level and then cover with a layer of breadcrumb mixture. Repeat the layers twice more, ending with a breadcrumb layer. Bake for 20 minutes, or until the top is golden brown. Cool in pan on a wire rack for about 30 minutes.

Spread the yogurt over the top of pudding. Remove the ring from the spring-form pan and serve immediately.

Nutrient Value:

Calories:	254	Cholesterol:	34.7 mg
Protein:	5.17 g	Fiber:	3.88 g
Carbohydrates:	58.4 g	% Fat Calories:	6
Total Fat:	1.77 g		

Peaches

History: China is believed to be the original home of the peach, the peach tree was considered the symbol of long life.

Nutrition: Peaches contain lots of vitamin A, and also vitamin C and minerals. For all it's healthfulness a medium size peach has only 38 calories.

Yield: There are 4 - 6 peaches to a pound.

Selecting: A glowing blush is not an indication that the peach is ripe - or even that it will taste good. A creamy yellow background is the best indication of a ripe and flavorful peach. A mellow fruit will also smell "peachy". Select peaches that give a little when squeezed gently.

When buying canned peaches, look for those whose labels list the drained weight instead of net weight, or you may be buying too much liquid. Always buy fruit that is in it's own juice with no added sugar.

Storing: Peaches should be stored at room temperature until soft enough to eat, then refrigerate and use as soon as you can.

Peachy Tips:

Peaches and cream: Mix together nonfat yogurt with a little brown sugar, and use as a topping on fresh peaches.

Peaches to drink: Mix together plain nonfat yogurt, sliced fresh peaches, wheat germ bran, a little honey or sugar, and skim or low fat milk. Blend well.

A Peachy Extra: Peaches are a great garnish for ham, pork or poultry. Cut peaches into slices, and place in fan shape at the side of the meat.

Peach Cobbler

This is a very good recipe that can be made with either fresh peaches, or canned peaches in their own juice.

Serves 6

4 cups peeled and sliced ripe peaches
8 tablespoons granulated sugar
grated rind (zest) of 1 large lemon
1-2 tablespoons fresh lemon juice
1/2 teaspoon almond extract
1/2 cup whole wheat pastry flour, sifted
1 cup all purpose flour, sifted
1 tablespoon baking powder
1/2 teaspoon salt
5 tablespoons unsalted butter
1 egg white lightly beaten
1/4 cup skim milk
1 tablespoon sugar (optional) for sprinkling

Method

Preheat oven to 400 degrees. Lightly spray a 2 quart baking dish with cooking spray.

Arrange peaches in the bottom of the dish and sprinkle with 6 tablespoons sugar, lemon zest, juice, and almond extract. Bake for 20 minutes, uncovered.

Meanwhile, in a food processor or electric mixer, combine the sifted flours, remaining 2 tablespoons sugar, baking powder, and salt. Cut in the cold butter until mixture resembles dry cornmeal. Add the beaten egg white and milk until just combined.

Remove peaches from oven, and drop large spoonfulls of dough over surface. Sprinkle with optional tablespoon of sugar and return to oven for 15 - 20 minutes, or until top is firm and golden brown.

Serve hot, with one of the whipped cream recipes if desired.

Nutrient Value:

Calories:	307	Cholesterol:	26.1 mg
Protein:	4.99 g	Fiber:	3.29 g
Carbohydrates:	51.5 g	% Fat Calories:	29
Total Fat:	10.1 g		

Fresh Peach Betty

This delicious peach recipe is quick and easy to make. Use the sweetest, ripest fruit you can find.

Serves 8

8 medium-sized peaches (about 2 pounds)
2 cups soft whole wheat bread crumbs
2/3 cup sugar
2 tablespoons whole wheat pastry flour
pinch salt
2 tablespoons butter

Method:

Preheat oven to 375 degrees. Lightly spray a 2-quart casserole with cooking spray.

Slice peaches and place half in the casserole. Combine breadcrumbs, sugar, flour and salt. Top peaches with half of this mixture. Dot with 1 tablespoon butter or margerine. Repeat layering with remaining peaches and breadcrumbs.

Bake about 40 minutes or until crumbs are golden and peaches are tender.

Nutrient Values:

Calories:	177	Cholesterol:	7.77 mg
Protein:	2.01 g	Fiber:	2.40 g
Carbohydrates:	36.5 g	% Fat Calories:	17
Total Fat:	3.46 g		

Fresh Fruit Salad

This fruit salad is one of my favorites, and I also use it whenever I make my English Trifle recipe. It keeps for several days, refrigerated. Vary the fruit according to the season.

Serves 10

2 pears, peeled and diced
2 red delicious apples, unpeeled, and diced
2 small bananas, not too ripe, sliced
1 small can mandarin oranges, including the juice
1 cup seedless grapes
1 cup strawberries, sliced
1 cup frozen blackberries
3/4 cup water
3/4 cup sweet white wine
1/4 cup orange juice
2 tablespoons lemon juice
2 tablespoons Triple-sec or Grand Marnier (optional)
grated rind from 1 very large orange
1/2 cup sugar

Method

Before you begin to cut up the fruit make the following: in a small non-aluminum saucepan mix together water, wine, orange juice, lemon juice, Grand Marnier or Triple-Sec, rind and 1/2 cup sugar. Heat until sugar is dissolved, stirring once or twice. Cool slightly, and pour into a large glass bowl.

Cut up the fruit and place into glass bowl with the liquid. Cover, refrigerate for several hours to allow fruit to macerate.

VARIATION: English Trifle fruit salad; Leave out wine, Triple-Sec or Grand Marnier. Substitute another 3/4 cup water (total 1 1/2 cups water), and an extra 2 tablespoons lemon juice, (making 4 tablespoons in all).

Nutrient Values:

Calories:	179	Cholesterol:	0 mg
Protein:	1.03 g	Fiber:	4.37 g
Carbohydrates:	40.6 g	% Fat Calories:	3
Total Fat:	0.634 g		

Strawberries

Selecting: Look for strawberries whose caps are bright green and attached. Brown caps indicate aging fruit.

Storing: Never wash berries before storing them in the refrigerator. They will stay fresh much longer.

Preparing: Well chilled berries are less likely to become mushy when washed. Wash berries with the caps on, otherwise water will get into the berries and dilute the flavor, and make the strawberries mushy.

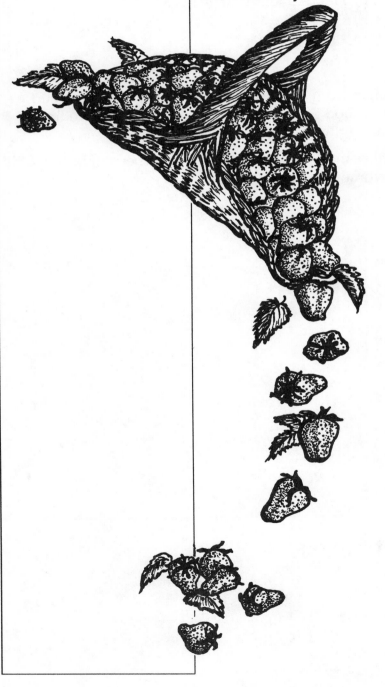

Strawberry Yogurt Whip

This light and fluffy dessert can be made in advance or just before serving.

Serves 4

1/2 pint strawberries
1 1/4 cups nonfat yogurt
grated rind of 1 orange
1 tablespoon honey or sugar
2 teaspoons powdered gelatin
    dissolved in 3 tablespoons orange juice
2 egg whites

Method

Reserve enough fresh berries for garnish. Puree the strawberries in a blender or food processor. Add the remaining ingredients except for the egg whites and blend for 2 seconds.

Beat egg whites until stiff. Fold into the strawberry mixture. Chill until set. Decorate with a strawberry.

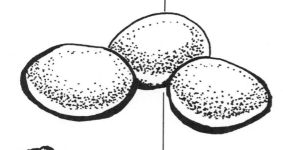

Nutrient Values:

Calories:	114	Cholesterol:	0 mg
Protein:	4.97 g	Fiber:	0.519 g
Carbohydrates:	24.1 g	% Fat Calories:	0
Total Fat:	0.057 g		

Strawberry Yogurt Crunch

This is a very pleasant dessert that is also high in fiber.

Serves 4

1 envelope unflavored gelatin
1 cup boiling water
2 cups strawberry or plain nonfat yogurt
1 pint strawberries, rinsed, patted dry, and hulled
2 tablespoons honey
1 teaspoon pure vanilla extract
3 ounces ready to eat granola type cereal

Method

In a blender or food processor, put strawberries, yogurt, honey, and vanilla. Blend 30 seconds on high. Mixture should be a thick puree. add boiling water and gelatin, and blend for 10 seconds more. Place in large parfait glasses, or serving dishes and chill for at least 30 minutes. Just before serving top with 3/4 oz granola type cereal.

VARIATIONS: Blueberries or any other fruit can be substituted for the strawberries, and the yogurt flavor can be changed to match the fruit you choose.

Nutrient Values:

Calories:	183	Cholesterol:	2.00 mg
Protein:	9.80 g	Fiber:	4.30 g
Carbohydrates:	32.5 g	% Fat Calories:	12
Total Fat:	2.46 g		

Your Notes:

Chocolate Pound Cake

This delicious, moist cake, is one of our favorites. It is good served plain or with one of the fruit sauces topped with mock whipped cream (see pages 45-50). Be sure the cake is cold before cutting it.

Makes 20 slices

6 tablespoons butter
1 1/4 cups sugar
3 eggs, beaten
1/2 cup cocoa, sifted
2 cups flour, sifted
1 cup low fat buttermilk
1 1/2 teaspoons baking soda
1 1/2 teaspoons pure vanilla extract
1/2 teaspoon almond extract

Method

Preheat oven to 350° degrees.

In a food processor or electric mixer, cream together butter, sugar and eggs until light. Add the cocoa and mix well. Add the flour alternately with buttermilk, blending well. Stir in soda, vanilla, and almond extract, mixing just until smooth. Do not overmix!

Spread batter in a 9 x 5 x 3 inch non-stick loaf pan that has been lightly sprayed with cooking spray.

Bake at 350 degrees for 50-60 minutes, or until a toothpick inserted in the center of the loaf comes out clean, and the top of the loaf springs back when lightly touched.Do not overbake!

Cool in the pan on a wire rack for 10 minutes. Turn out the cake and cool completely before serving.

Nutrient Values:

Calories:	143	Cholesterol:	50.9 mg
Protein:	2.93 g	Fiber:	0.950 g
Carbohydrates:	22.9 g	% Fat Calories:	30
Total Fat:	4.92 g		

Chocolate Angel Food Cake

Light and airy, this cake is wonderful either plain, or with sliced strawberries and nonfat yogurt. It is also good with frozen yogurt and fresh fruit. The white variation is great to use when making an "English Trifle"

Serves 12

3/4 cup cake flour
1 1/2 cups sugar
1/4 cup cocoa
13 egg whites
2 teaspoons cream of tartar
1/4 teaspoon salt
1 1/2 teaspoons pure vanilla extract
1/2 teaspoon almond extract

Method

Pre-heat oven to 375 degres. Adjust oven rack so it is one third of the way up from the bottom.

Sift flour, 3/4 cup sugar, and cocoa together <u>three times</u>, set aside.

Whip egg whites until they are foamy. Add cream of tartar, salt, vanilla and almond extract. Beat until stiff buy not dry. Add 3/4 cup sugar slowly, a tablespoon at a time, beating well after each addition until well blended. Blend beaten egg whites in three stages. Be sure the flour is well incorporated, but do not overwork the mixture.

Pour into ungreased 10 inch angel food cake pan. Pull metal knife through batter twice to break up large air bubbles. Bake at 375 degrees for 35 - 45 minutes. Test for doneness after 30 minutes by inserting a thin wooden skewer into the middle of the cake. The skewer should come out with no trace of raw batter on it. When the cake is done, remove from oven and invert pan over the neck of a bottle to cool.

VARIATION: For a plain white cake, omit the cocoa powder and add an additional 1/4 cup cake flour.

Nutrient Values:

Calories:	144	Cholesterol:	0 mg
Protein:	4.70 g	Fiber:	0.727 g
Carbohydrates:	31.7 g	% Fat Calories:	2
Total Fat:	0.413 g		

No Superfine Sugar:
Make your own by processing regular sugar in the blender until fine.

Chocolate Meringues

Makes about 60 small meringues

3 egg whites
1/2 teaspoon cream of tartar
1 cup sugar (superfine if possible)
3 tablespoons cocoa, (preferably Dutch processed), unsweetened

Method

Preheat oven to 250 degrees.

Separate the eggs from the yolks being very careful that not a trace of yolk gets into the whites, beat in a medium bowl until foamy. Add the cream of tartar. Continue beating until soft peaks form, and then very slowly beat in the sugar 1 tablespoon at a time until stiff. Fold in the cocoa. Drop batter by tablespoonsful onto non-stick cookie sheets sprayed with cooking spray, or cookie sheets lined with parchment paper. Bake for 30 minutes. Turn oven off, and leave meringues in oven for at least 2 hours, or preferably overnight. Remove from pans. Store in a dry place.

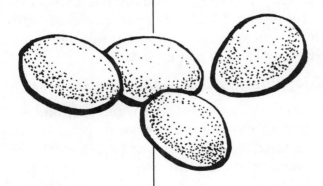

Nutrient Values:

Calories:	8.60	Cholesterol:	0 mg
Protein:	0.128 g	Fiber:	0.048 g
Carbohydrates:	2.08 g	% Fat Calories:	3
Total Fat:	0.031 g		

Baking:
Before baking a cake, rap the pans sharply on the counter top before placing in the oven, this will help eliminate air bubbles.

Cinnamon Coffee Cake

This delightful moist cake is easy to make, and keeps for several days.

Serves 12

1 cup nonfat yogurt
1 teaspoon baking soda
1 1/2 cups whole wheat blend flour
2 teaspoons baking powder
4 tablespoons unsalted butter
1 cup brown sugar
1 egg
1 teaspoon vanilla

<u>Topping</u>

1/2 cup brown sugar
1 tablespoon cinnamon

Method

Lightly spray a 10 inch non-stick bundt pan with cooking spray. Preheat oven to 350 degrees.

Sift together flour and baking powder. Set aside.

In a small bowl, combine yogurt and baking soda; mix well and set aside. (The mixture will increase in volume.)

In a food processor or electric mixer, beat together the butter and sugar until well mixed. Add the egg and vanilla, and beat until very light and fluffy — about 2-3 minutes in an electric mixer, or 30 seconds in a food processor. Add the flour mixture alternately with yogurt mixture, only until just mixed.

Mix together the topping ingredients, and set aside.

Spread half the batter in the prepared pan, and sprinkle with half the topping. Cover with remaining batter, and sprinkle with remaining topping. Bake for 45 minutes or until a toothpick inserted in the center comes out clean. Remove from oven, and place on a wire rack to cool for 10 minutes. Remove from bundt pan, inverting onto wire rack, and allow to cool completely.

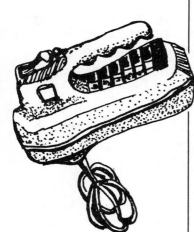

Nutrient Values:

Calories:	209	Cholesterol:	33.5 mg
Protein:	3.47 g	Fiber:	1.29 g
Carbohydrates:	39.9 g	% Fat Calories:	19
Total Fat:	4.58 g		

Cinnamon Applesauce Cake

This delicious cake is very moist and keeps well. It looks most attractive when made in a bundt pan, and can be sprinkled with a small amount of powdered sugar when cool.

Serves 16

1 3/4 cups granulated sugar
4 tablespoons butter, at room temperature
1 egg
1/2 cup nonfat yogurt
2 cups applesauce
1 teaspoon orange extract
1 teaspoon vanilla
2-3/4 cups whole wheat blend flour
3 tablespoons bran
2 teaspoons cinnamon
2 teaspoons baking soda
1 cup raisins
powdered sugar (optional)

Method

Preheat oven to 325 degrees.

Lightly spray a non-stick bundt pan with cooking spray.

In a food processor or electric mixer, combine sugar and butter, and mix well. Add the egg and beat until light in color. Add the yogurt, mixing well to incorporate throroughly, and then add applesauce, orange extract and vanilla.

In a separate bowl combine the flour, bran, cinnamon, baking soda, and raisins. Stir well to mix. Add the dry ingredients to the applesauce mixture, and stir only until just incorporated. Do not overmix the batter at this stage.

Pour into the prepared pan, and bake in the oven for 80 - 90 minutes, or until a toothpick inserted in the center comes out clean. Remove from oven, let cool in pan on a wire rack for 20 minutes, then remove from pan, and place on rack to finish cooling completely. Do not cut until cool. Sprinkle with powdered sugar if desired.

Nutrient Values:

Calories:	238	Cholesterol:	25.0 mg
Protein:	3.78 g	Fiber:	2.95 g
Carbohydrates:	50.0 g	% Fat Calories:	13
Total Fat:	3.64 g		

Instant "Ice Cream"

This is a very good substitute for ice-cream and is low in fat and calories. You need a food processor in order to make this, as the fruit must be frozen. Be sure to try this recipe!

Serves 6

1/4 cup nonfat yogurt, either plain,
    or match the flavor with the fruit you are using
2 egg whites
3 cups frozen fruit, (peaches, strawberries, raspberries, etc.)
2 tablespoons sugar, or sugar substitute
2 teaspoons lemon juice

Method

Place yogurt, egg whites, sugar and lemon juice in the food processor. Blend briefly. With the processor running, gradually add the frozen fruit pieces until soft "ice cream" is formed - approximately 2-3 minutes. Serve immediately.

Nutrient Values:

Calories:	53.1	Cholesterol:	0.167 mg
Protein:	1.98 g	Fiber:	1.94 g
Carbohydrates:	12.0 g	% Fat Calories:	2
Total Fat:	0.102 g		

English Trifle

This is one of my favorite recipes, adapted from the high fat, calorie laden original, I had been making since I was 10 years old.

Serves 10

1/2 trifle fruit salad recipe (see page 256)
1/2 angel food cake
1/2 cup sweet sherry (optional)
1/4 cup low-calorie raspberry jam
1 packet low-calorie vanilla pudding (not instant)
1 recipe whipped cream topping (see pages 46-7), or low calorie
　　whipped cream substitute

Method

Split angel food cake in half, horizontally and spread with jam. Cut into large cubes, and place in bottom and half way up the sides of a large glass serving bowl. Sprinkle with 1/2 cup sweet sherry, then add the prepared fruit salad. Set aside.

Make pudding according to package directions, using low fat milk. Cool, until able to pour over the fruit salad, cover and refrigerate until very cold.

Make whipped cream topping and either spread or pipe through a large pastry tip over the top of the pudding layer. Individual trifles can also be made in dishes made for this purpose, or else use individual glass bowls.

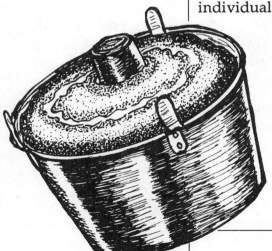

Nutrient Values:

Calories:	362	Cholesterol:	12.6 mg
Protein:	8.27 g	Fiber:	2.80 g
Carbohydrates:	72.3 g	% Fat Calories:	9
Total Fat:	3.64 g		

Honey Hermits

Hermit recipes go back hundreds of years, and originated during the days of the clipper ships. Because these cookies kept well for several weeks, they endured the ship voyages.

Makes about 30 cookies

1 1/4 cups whole wheat flour
1/2 teaspoon baking soda
1/2 teaspoon cinnamon
1/2 teaspoon allspice
1/4 teaspoon nutmeg
1/4 teaspoon salt
4 tablespoons unsalted butter
4 tablespoons light brown sugar, firmly packed
1/2 cup honey
1 egg
1 1/2 tablespoons 2% milk
1/2 cup raisins
1/2 cup pitted dates, coarsely chopped
1/2 cup walnut pieces

Method

Preheat oven to 400 degrees. Line cookie sheets with aluminum foil.

Sift together flour, baking soda, spices, and salt, and set aside.

In an electric mixer or food processor cream together the butter and sugar until light and fluffy. Add the honey, egg, and milk, and beat well. Add the dry ingredients gradually, and beat until just mixed. By hand, stir in the raisins, dates, and walnuts.

Drop by heaping teaspoonfulls of dough onto the lined cookie sheets, and bake for 10-12 minutes or until brown, and tops barely spring back when lightly touched with a fingertip. Remove to wire racks to cool.

Nutrient Values:

Calories:	86.7	Cholesterol:	13.3 mg
Protein:	1.37 g	Fiber:	1.17 g
Carbohydrates:	14.8 g	% Fat Calories:	30
Total Fat:	3.11 g		

Chocolate Raisin Cookies

These cookies are thin, large, and soft-chewy. Watch them carefully so they do not overcook.

Makes 42 cookies

1 3/4 cups all-purpose flour
1 teaspoon double-acting baking powder
1/2 teaspoon baking soda
1/4 teaspoon salt
4 tablespoons cocoa
1 cup raisins
8 tablespoons butter
1 teaspoon vanilla extract
1 1/3 cups granulated sugar
1 egg
1/2 cup nonfat yogurt

Method

Preheat oven to 375 degrees. Line the cookie sheets with foil.

Sift together the flour, baking powder, baking soda, salt, and cocoa, set aside.

In an electric mixer or food processor, cream the butter and vanilla extract. Add the sugar and beat well. Add the egg and yogurt, and continue to beat until well mixed. Gradually beat in the dry ingredients, scraping the bowl well with a rubber spatula, but only beating until mixed. Stir in the raisins.

Using a heaping teaspoonful of dough for each cookie, place the dough 2-3 inches apart on the prepared cookie sheets.

Bake for 12-15 minutes or until tops spring back when lightly pressed. Be carful not to overbake. These cookies should be slightly soft and chewy in the centers with crisp edges. Overbaking will make the cookies hard.

Nutrient Values:

Calories:	79.4	Cholesterol:	12.5 mg
Protein:	1.08 g	Fiber:	0.524 g
Carbohydrates:	13.9 g	% Fat Calories:	27
Total Fat:	2.50 g		

Oatmeal Raisin Cookies

Makes 72 cookies

12 tablespoons butter
3/4 cup granulated sugar
3/4 cup firmly packed brown sugar
2 eggs
1 teaspoon vanilla
3/4 cup all-purpose flour
3/4 cup whole wheat flour
1 teaspoon baking soda
1/2 teaspoon salt
2 cups quick cooking rolled oats
12 ounces raisins

Method

Preheat oven 350 degrees. Line cookie sheets with foil

Beat butter and sugars until light and creamy. Beat in the eggs and vanilla. In a separate bowl stir together both flours, baking soda, and salt. Add to the creamed mixture beating only until incorporated. Stir in the oats and raisins.

Bake for 10 - 12 minutes or until golden brown. Remove cookie sheets from oven and place on wire racks for a few mintes to cool slightly. Remove cookies from cookie sheets to wire racks and cool.

Nutrient Values:

Calories:	67.4	Cholesterol:	12.8 mg
Protein:	1.01 g	Fiber:	0.715 g
Carbohydrates:	11.4 g	% Fat Calories:	29
Total Fat:	2.27 g		

Crunchy Granola Cookies

These delicious, crunchy cookies, keep well, and are full of vitamins and minerals.

Makes about 6 dozen cookies

2 cups all-purpose flour
1 teaspoon baking soda
1/2 teaspoon baking powder
1/2 teaspoon salt
12 tablespoons butter, at room temperature
3/4 cup granulated sugar
3/4 cup firmly packed brown sugar
2 eggs
1 teaspoon vanilla
2 cups granola
1 1/2 cups slightly crushed wheat flakes
1/3 cup wheat germ
1 cup raisins

Method

Preheat oven to 350 degrees. Line cookie sheets with foil, and set aside.

Stir together the flour, baking soda, baking powder, and salt.

In a food processor or electric mixer beat together the butter and sugars until light and creamy. Beat in the eggs and vanilla. Add the flour mixture, and beat only until well incorporated. By hand, mix in the granola, crushed wheat flakes, wheat germ, and raisins.

Drop by rounded teaspoonfulls onto the cookie sheets. Flatten slightly with a fork. Bake in a 350 degree oven for 10 - 12 minutes, or until golden brown. Remove immediately to wire racks to cool.

Nutrient Values:

Calories:	77.8	Cholesterol:	12.8 mg
Protein:	1.18 g	Fiber:	0.883 g
Carbohydrates:	13.0 g	% Fat Calories:	30

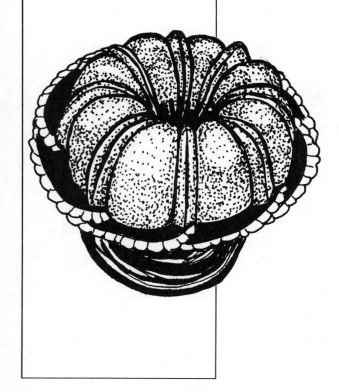

272

Sample Menus

Breakfast Ideas

Juice
Strawberry Blintz Omelette
Whole Wheat Lahvosh
Coffee or Tea

Juice
Blackberry Cobbler
Coffee or Tea

Fresh Peach Shake
Irish Soda Bread
Coffee or Tea

Strawberry Yogurt Drink
Whole Wheat Lahvosh
Coffee or Tea

Orange Milkshake
Apple Raisin Muffins
Coffee or Tea

Banana Shake
Banana and Apple Loaf
Coffee or Tea

Blackberry Apple Spritzer
Pumpkin Raisin Muffins
Coffee or Tea

Sample Menus

Lunch Ideas

Island Seafood Salad
Whole Wheat Roll
Assorted Cookies

Turkey in French Rolls
Salad of assorted raw vegetables
Fresh Fruit Salad

Pasta Primavera
Strawberry Yogurt Crunch

Southwest Vegetable Soup
Irish Soda Bread

Chicken and Capellini Soup
Whole Wheat Bread
Fresh Fruit

Vegetarian Stuffed Peppers
Peach Betty

Ratatouille
Banana Blackberry Mousse

Sample Menus

Dinner Ideas

Chicken Fajitas
Spicy Beans
Tomato Salsa with Papayas and Pears
Nonfat yogurt
Instant "Ice Cream"

Stuffed Clams
Baked Cabbage with Chestnuts
Apple Pudding

Hot and Sour Soup
Chinese Stir-Fried Chicken
Bananas with Pineapple Rum Sauce

Red Snapper with Red Peppers,
Onions, and White Wine
Brown Rice
Salad
Chocolate Pound Cake

Pasta with Bay Scallops
Tossed Salad
English Trifle

Seafood Gazpacho
Barbecue Chicken with Mangoes
 and Mustard Relish
Strawberry Yogurt Crunch

Zucchini Stuffed with Crabmeat
Vegetable Lasagna with Fresh Herbs
Fruit Salad

Index

Index

Index

Index

Index

Index

Index